Operational Faith

A Guide to Discovering God's Will for Your Life

DR. DERRIUS M. COLVIN SR.

authorHOUSE®

AuthorHouse™
1663 Liberty Drive
Bloomington, IN 47403
www.authorhouse.com
Phone: 1 (800) 839-8640

Published by AuthorHouse 03/01/2019

ISBN: 978-1-5462-7859-7 (sc)
ISBN: 978-1-5462-7858-0 (hc)
ISBN: 978-1-5462-7857-3 (e)

Library of Congress Control Number: 2019901210

Print information available on the last page.

To my wife, Anita, with whom I have been blessed to share a journey of love for over thirty-four years

Contents

Preface

Many Christians have an idea of what faith is from the many lessons and sermons on the subject. However, the question is: Does the faith community really operate their lives by faith? This book is written to help both new and mature Christians, as well as pastors, become spiritually stronger. It attempts to go beyond just talking about faith (and occasionally using it) to helping the Christian learn how to live by faith … to operate his or her life by faith.

In this book, I introduce the Model of Faith, a guide to help the believer utilize operational faith in every area of his or her life. Throughout the various chapters, I will explore God's will and the path that a Christian should take to discover God's will for his or her life by utilizing operational faith. I will also explore the relationship between God's will, the voice of God, obedience, operational faith, prayer, and patience. In addition, I will discuss that when we do the will of God, God grants our request for blessings in our lives.

At the end of each chapter are discussion questions that are intended to help the believer put into action what he or she has learned. In the appendix, I have also included sermons relating to operational faith. All scripture references are English Standard Version, unless otherwise noted.

Operational faith is not meant to be separate from the other spiritual virtues mentioned in scripture, but rather it is connected to them. In particular, operational faith is connected to hearing the voice of God. As a Christian, our faith moves forward because of what God has said, and it leads to the completion of God's will in the believer's life. Faith has helpers, prayer, and patience, which support it in overcoming obstacles that would otherwise quench it.

As you read this book, be prayerful and allow the Holy Spirit to speak to you and guide you to fully understand the power of growing your faith. I encourage you to utilize a notebook to answer the discussion questions and to write down notes to reference as you read each chapter. Remember, living by faith pleases God.

"And without faith it is impossible to please him, for whoever would draw near to God must believe that he exists and that he rewards those who seek him" (Hebrews 11:6).

Acknowledgments

I praise and thank God for allowing me the opportunity to finish writing this book. The Lord put it on my heart to write many years ago. The journey has included many challenging experiences. Yet, with his help, he has allowed me to complete it, as well as, to step out on faith regarding how it would be published and promoted. To God be the glory for all the things he has done!

I would like to thank the following people for their support in this project. Dr. Joseph B. Felker, Jr., my spiritual father in the ministry, encouraged and provided guidance from the time I was a young boy to my calling as a minister of the gospel.

My family, starting with my wife, Anita, has been with me throughout this entire journey as a source of strength, support, and love, and she offered her editorial assistance. My mother, Delores Colvin, set the standard on demonstrating unconditional love to my sisters and I. Thanks to my children—DeAnna, Dañelle, and Derrius Jr.—for their prayers and love.

My First Progressive Church family allowed me the opportunity to teach and preach to them, which helped me to utilize the principles of operational faith on a weekly basis.

Operational Faith

"Have I yet found myself in God's will?

Have I yet lost myself in His Trust?

Is my faith solid in going forward where I cannot see?"

Dr. Derrius M. Colvin Sr.

THE MODEL OF FAITH

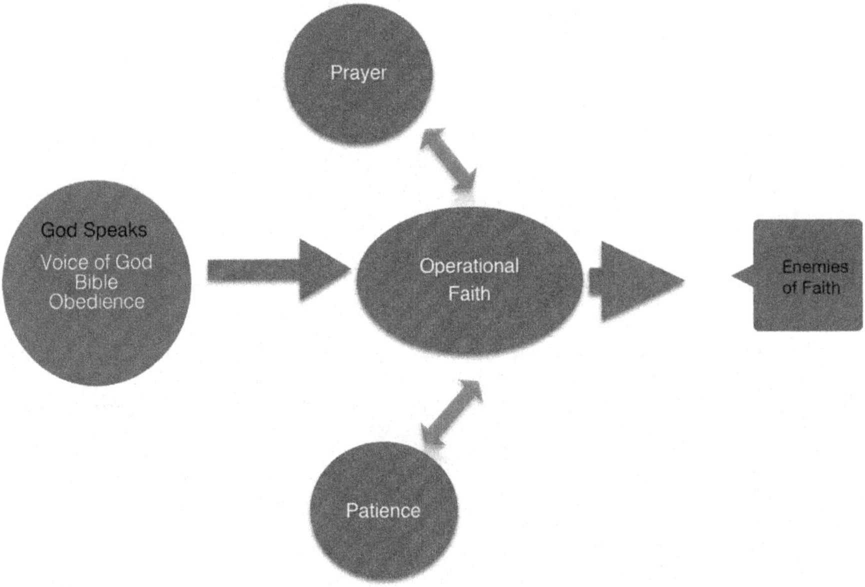

Part I

Learning to Operate Your Life by Faith

Chapter 1

Understanding God's Will: Part 1

Do not be conformed to this world, but be transformed by the renewal of your mind, that by testing you may discern what is the will of God, what is good and acceptable and perfect.

—Romans 12:2

In 2007, my wife and I boarded a train from Chicago to Fargo, North Dakota. Our only son had gotten injured playing college football, so we felt it necessary to go in person and check on his condition. During our journey, the train made several stops. It went fast in the open fields and slowly as it entered the various train stations. We wanted the train to make only one stop, Fargo, because we were anxious to reach our destination. Although we prayed and put our trust in God, we still had to deal with the temptation of worrying and becoming impatient. Our minds were on our son's condition, and we were hoping to get to him as quickly as possible. After thirteen hours and 670 miles, we finally arrived.

Every day, many Christians wonder what God's will is for their lives. There are those who believe that if they go to church every Sunday, they are doing the will of God, as if the act of attending church is the only thing that God requires. There are others, however, who believe that God's will involves more than simply attending Sunday worship. Many of these Christians are searching diligently to discover God's will for their lives. Some believe that it is God's will for them to preach, sing in the choir, conduct missionary work, or teach Sunday school. Yet there are many Christians serving in leadership positions within their church who are still uncertain as to whether they are doing the will of God.

Discerning God's Will

How do we discover God's will for our lives? To fully understand it, we must first have a proper understanding of the Word of God. In addition, we must develop a close relationship with God through prayer and obedience-driven lifestyles.

What does the Word of God say about God's will? How does a Christian determine God's will for his or her life? Is everything that happens in a Christian's life the will of God? Some Christians believe that it's too difficult to know what God's will is, so they fail to make any attempt to find out. There are those who interpret Romans 8:28 ("And we know that for those who love God all things work together for good, for those who are called according to his purpose") to mean that whatever happens to them must be the will of God because he allowed it to happen. Later we will take a further look at this scripture and how it pertains to the will of God.

What is God's will? The will of God is found in God's Word, the Bible. God's Holy Scriptures reveal God's will to humankind. God's will is also revealed through his spoken Word. Jesus revealed the Father's will when he communicated with man on earth. God's will was disclosed through the voice of Jesus. The Holy Spirit spoke to writers in both the Old and New Testaments to write God's will. If you are going to discover God's will for your life, you must begin to study, not just read, God's Word. Let me say this again for emphasis: if you are going to discover God's will for your life, you must study *and not just read* God's Word.

The Bible: The Key to God's Will

According to a LifeWay research study,

> Only 45 percent of those who regularly attend church read the Bible more than once a week. Over 40 percent of the people attending read their Bible occasionally, maybe once or twice a month. Almost 1 in 5 churchgoers say they never read the Bible—essentially the same number who read it every day.[1]

If you want to discover where in God's vineyard he wants you to serve, you must study the Bible. As you grow spiritually in the Word of God, the Holy Spirit can speak to you concerning what it is he wants you to do. Seeking to discover the will of God also means understanding that God wants to have a personal relationship with you. He wants you to develop a love relationship with him.

To say it plainly and simply, he wants you to love him with everything you have (all your heart) and then love those who are around you—both friend and enemy. You must live this love, and in doing so, you're doing the will of God. God will reveal to us what his will is for our lives as we continue to grow in his Word. We put ourselves in the path of discovering God's will as we study God's Word and develop our relationship with him.

Since the Bible reveals the will of God, it is important to know that God wants all humankind to discover who he is. We must learn that God is our Creator and Redeemer. We must learn all we can about Jesus and believe he is our Savior. According to Luke 19:10, Jesus came to save the lost. The apostle John summed up the ministry of Jesus as follows: "But these are written so that you may believe that Jesus is the Christ, the Son of God, and that by believing you may have life in his name" (John 20:31). If you have never repented of your sins nor confessed Jesus as your Lord and Savior, you cannot move forward in discovering the

---

[1] "The Epidemic of Bible Illiteracy in Our Churches," https://www.christianitytoday.com/edstetzer/2015/july/epidemic-of-bible-illiteracy-in-our-churches.html

will of God until you have experienced the grace of God. God tells us through his servant Paul, "For by grace you have been saved through faith. And this is not your own doing; it is the gift of God, not a result of works, so that no one may boast" (Ephesian 2:8–9).

I encourage you to become a Christian, and then you can move to the next level of discovering the will of God. There is no greater decision in your life than to accept Jesus Christ as your Lord and Savior.

Completing the Will of God

After we discover what God wants us to do in life, we must then understand the importance of completing God's will. We must not start and then stop; we must run the Christian race until he tells us, "Well done." Just as the goal for a runner in a marathon is not simply to start the race but to complete it, we as Christians should aim to successfully complete our race.

As Christians, we are to discover God's will for our lives by faith and then operate our lives by faith to complete the will of God. When my wife and I traveled on the train to see our son, our mission was to reach our destination and to find out about his condition. We did not want to settle for anything short of our goal. We wanted to see our son. When we are in God's will, our desire must be to complete God's mission for our lives.

The Bible gives examples of men and women who discovered the will of God for their lives and completed it. Four examples are Moses, Esther, Paul, and Jesus. I will discuss each one's journey and how each operated within God's will. Moses discovered God's will for his life when he saw a burning bush that was not consumed. God captured Moses's attention by attracting him to a mountain and then having a conversation with him.

Not only did Moses discover that God was real, he also learned that God had a mission for him. The mission entailed going back to Egypt and telling Pharaoh that the Lord wanted him to release the Israelites from their captivity. The mission further involved Moses leading the children of Israel out of Egypt and into the wilderness.

All along the way, Moses would have to utilize his faith to keep him moving forward. God's will for Moses was for him to bring the children of Israel to the edge of the Promised Land. Although Moses himself was not allowed to enter, he completed God's will for his life. In chapter 4, we will discuss how Moses utilized prayer to help him in his journey of completing God's will.

God's name is not mentioned in the book of Esther, yet his divine presence is seen throughout the book. Esther was a woman who certainly was doing the will of God. It was by God's providence that Esther was the queen at a right time when her people needed her the most. Esther cared deeply for her people and used her faith to take her forward. She was determined that she must go to the king. So she declared that the Jews should fast with her for three days, knowing if she went to the king without him requesting her to come that she could face death. She spoke memorable words when she said, "Then I will go to the king, though it is against the law, and if I perish, I perish" (Esther 4:16). Esther was doing the will of God and in the process saved her people.

The apostle Paul is another biblical example of a man who discovered God's will for his life and completed it. Paul first thought he was doing God's will when he was arresting Jewish Christians residing in Jerusalem. However, as he was making his way to the city of Damascus to arrest more Christians, he saw a shining light and heard the voice of Jesus. Through this experience, Paul's life became connected to God's will. The Lord revealed to him that he was to be a witness to the Gentiles. Paul utilized great faith, which helped him to complete God's will for his life. This involved establishing churches and preaching and teaching to Jews and Gentiles on three missionary journeys. Many of his travels involved personal sufferings and much persecution.

Still Paul completed the will of God for his life by being a witness for the Lord to those who did not know Jesus in Rome. Paul summarized his life in a statement to his spiritual son Timothy, "I have fought the good fight, I have finished the race, I have kept the faith" (2 Timothy 4:7).

The fourth and arguably best example of a man completing the will of God is Jesus Christ. I like to call our Savior the prototype of a person who is totally in the will of God. Jesus began his public ministry by being baptized by John the Baptist in the Jordan River. "Then Jesus was led up by the Spirit into the wilderness to be tempted by the devil" (Matthew 4:1).

The person who is in the will of God is a person who is being led totally by the Holy Spirit. The Holy Spirit both leads and empowers the believer. Jesus's entire ministry was in the will of God. Jesus made it clear to his disciples what his mission was. "For I have come down from heaven, not to do my own will but the will of him who sent me" (John 6:38).

God's will for Jesus was not only to declare himself to the world by healing the sick, raising the dead, preaching to the poor, and feeding the hungry, but it was also God's will for Jesus to die for the sins of the world and then be resurrected with the power of God. Jesus says, "For this is the will of my Father, that everyone who looks on the Son and believes in him should have eternal life, and I will raise him up on the last day" (John 6:40).

In the garden of Gethsemane, Jesus's focus was still on God's will despite the suffering that he would have to endure. He said, "Father, if you are willing, remove this cup from me. Nevertheless, not my will, but yours, be done" (Luke 22:42). From Jesus's baptism to his resurrection, his concern was to fulfill the Father's will, as outlined in scripture. The Old Testament prophets spoke of the Messiah coming into the world and the things he would accomplish.

Jesus was the Messiah, and he always did those things that pleased the Father. The prophet Isaiah wrote of the great suffering of Christ, how it was God's will when he said, "Yet it was the will of the Lord to crush him; he has put him to grief; when his soul makes an offering for guilt, he shall see his offspring; he shall prolong his days; the will of the Lord shall prosper in his hand" (Isaiah 53:10).

Jesus, in doing the Father's will, made the greatest sacrifice for us when he suffered and died for us. Jesus's suffering, death, and resurrection was all a part of the will of God. Jesus finished his Father's will when he stated on the cross, "It is finished"(John 19:30).

Let's look again at Romans 8:28 and see how this verse connects to the will of God. As Paul wrote, "And we know that for those who love God all things work together for good, for those who are called according to his purpose."

This verse describes a Christian who understands what it means to be in the will of God. What does this mean? Let me try to explain it this way. At the time that I am writing this book, my wife and I have three adult children, ages thirty-one, thirty, and twenty-nine. They grew up as stairsteps, right behind one another. When they were the age of four, five, and six, they would ride in the back seat of our station wagon playing with one another, talking, laughing, and just having plenty of fun. They were not worried about the cares of life. They did not ask us where we were driving them.

I believed that they trusted us even without fully understanding what trusting their parents meant. Many times they would fall asleep in the back seat of the car. When we reached our destination, we either woke them up or picked them up and carried them into the place we were going.

When we as Christians are in God's will, we love God as a child loves his or her parents, and we relax patiently in the back seat as God drives our lives. We don't express worry, anxiety, or fear because we know that the driver, our Father, is working together for our good according to his purpose. We totally rely on God to direct our path and order our footsteps.

Another way of understanding Romans 8:28 can be stated, "The Lord is guiding my life as I operate within my free will nature; because his Word is what commands my steps, therefore my destiny is determined by his divine will as I trust in him."

A second way of understanding Romans 8:28 is simply "my life is in the plan of God's will because my love for God motivates me to operate according to His word." When you understand Romans 8:28 in these ways, you understand that it does connect to the will of God. The central point is realizing the importance of loving God. So let me ask you: do you really love God?

Conclusion

Understanding God's will involves stepping onto the train of your life and allowing God to drive the train by directing you by faith to reach your destination. Every Christian should have a strong desire to be in the will of God. We must want God to lead our lives. We must put God first in our lives.

Whether you are a bus driver, secretary, plumber, or musician, you must honor your first calling, which is to live as a child of God. When you discover God and begin to seek those things that please him, you place yourself in the direct path of the will of God. God's will is about seeing the big picture from his point of view. God sees the beginning of our life at the same time he sees the end. The psalmist wrote, "The steps of a man are established by the Lord, when he delights in his way" (Psalm 37:23). Ecclesiastes 3:2a says "a time to be born, and a time to die." When we are in the will of God, we begin and end with God.

God wants you to discover his will for your life. The apostle Paul said it this way, "Therefore do not be foolish, but understand what the will of the Lord is" (Ephesians 5:17). For the best place for us to be is *in the will of God*. No matter where you live, whether it is in a war-torn country like Syria or relaxing on a peaceful beach in Honolulu, if we are in God's will, we will be in God's providence. When we understand the importance of being in the will of God, the next step is for us to be able to discern the voice of God. In the next chapter, I will explore ways to assist you in understanding the voice of God.

Discussion Questions/Exercises

1. How much time do you spend studying the Bible? Write a plan that you will follow to increase your study time. List the days of the week, the times, and the amount of time you will spend studying scripture.

2. Read the four gospels (Matthew, Mark, Luke, and John). Write down the highlights of each book to help you gain a better understanding of the life and ministry of Jesus. (If you have already read them, compare and contrast each book's view of Jesus as a way to get a deeper understanding of Jesus's life and ministry).

3. Explain what you believe to be God's will for your life. Write a one-page paper and discuss how your life has or has not been in the will of God. Include in the paper what you will do to get a better understanding of God's will. After you have completed this assignment, let a mature Christian read it and share with you their thoughts.

Chapter 2

Comprehending God's Voice (The Three Components)

It is written, "Man shall not live by bread alone, but by every word that comes from the mouth of God."

—Matthew 4:4

In chapter 1, we focused on the will of God. In chapter 2, I will present a model that depicts God's will. I call it the Model of Faith. The Model of Faith demonstrates how believers complete the will of God. It is a spiritual description that shows how a child of God can live his or her life in a way that pleases God in this present-day world. It is a tool that can be used to accomplish the will of God. The Model of Faith leads believers to God's blessings. Namely, when we as believers hear and obey God's voice, we walk in the direction in which God has told us. This leads us to the blessings of God. An example of this can be found in Psalm 37:4 where the psalmist wrote, "Delight yourself in the Lord, and he will give you the desires of your heart."

Another example is Jeremiah 7:23, where the prophet Jeremiah stated, "But this command I gave them: 'Obey my voice, and I will be your God, and you shall be my people. And walk in all the way that I command you, that it may be well with you.'"

Four spiritual principles make up the Model of Faith: God Speaks, Operational Faith, Prayer, and Patience. In this chapter, we will explore in detail the first spiritual principle, God Speaks, along with the three components that comprise this first principle, the Voice of God, the Bible (scripture), and Obedience.

God Speaks: An Overview

Every Christian should be in search of discerning the voice of God. Most people have a family member or a friend that they speak to every day. As Christians, hearing God speak to our heart must be our daily goal. Just like we speak to our family and friends, we should seek to be in conversation with God throughout the day. Before we can utilize our operational faith, we must first understand the importance of discerning how God speaks to his children. Our faith does not operate alone. It gets its commands from the voice of God.

God still speaks to his children in current times. He has always communicated with those he loves. In order to hear the voice of God, the first step is having a desire to hear his voice. If you are not expecting to hear the voice of God, you will not hear it. You can drown out God's calm, clear voice by the hustle and bustle of your everyday life.

It should also be noted that God may not speak to you the same way that a wife speaks to her husband or a police officer speaks to a motorist that he or she has just pulled over. Yet he can speak using these methods, if he chooses to do so. In scripture, God speaks to his followers through dreams, visions, angels, prophets/apostles, and other miraculous ways. Each of these can be classified as God speaking to his believers.

Some Christians allow their job, family, and social activities to dominate their time. As a result, few moments are left for quiet time with God. Begin to think about ways you can increase your moments with God by not allowing external activities to dominate all of your time. Recognize that it is God's desire to communicate with you.

Years ago, I began implementing what I call quiet time devotion (QTD). I strive daily to be in prayer by 5:30 a.m. I make my way to a quiet area in my home while my loved ones are still asleep, knowing that my Great King is awake, waiting for me to communicate with him. In the gospel of Luke, Jesus had QTD with the Father.

The Word says, "In these days he went out to the mountain to pray, and all night he continued in prayer to God" (Luke 6:12). Prayer is essential in activating your faith, so it is important that you try to increase your prayer time with God. Prayer will be discussed further in chapter 4.

In the twenty-first century, God is still communicating to his church. He knows how to speak directly to each believer. The question is: do we want to hear his voice? Do we want to do those things that will help us walk by faith because we have learned how to discern the voice of God?

After a long, hard day at work, I often sit on the couch and rest. At times the news might be on, and my grandchildren may be visiting. As I'm watching the news, I may ask my thirteen-year-old granddaughter to bring me a glass of orange juice from the refrigerator. She temporarily stops what she's doing, goes into the kitchen, takes the juice out of the refrigerator, pours the orange juice into a glass, and brings it to me. My granddaughter listened to my very words and obeyed them. She may have obeyed my words because I am an adult who has authority over her or because I was her papa, whom she knew loved her.

Either way, she was willing to obey me. In both scenarios, she listened and followed my instructions. I got my requested juice because there was someone who heard my voice, listened to me, and then followed my instructions. Hearing the voice of God is all about loving God as your Father and understanding what your heavenly Father is saying. In order to utilize operational faith, you must understand what God is saying, namely to discern and obey the voice of God.

One Sunday during worship service, I asked the congregation, "If God told you to do something, would you do it?" As I looked around the sanctuary, I noticed that 99 percent of the adult hands were raised, indicating that they would tell God, "Yes, they would do it." Yet so many Christians are not certain of what God is saying to them and thus misunderstand or ignore it. This is because they have not been trained or conditioned to hear the Lord's voice. You might be thinking that it is hard to understand what God is saying. Why doesn't he make it crystal clear for believers to hear his voice? God does make it clear, but we must be willing to get close to him in relationship to understand it.

In Mark 4, Jesus explained to his disciples the reason why he spoke to the people in parables. He stated that many of them would not otherwise understand his words because they were not really searching for the truth. However, he took time to explain the meaning of the parables to his true followers because they wanted to understand matters related to the kingdom of God.

For those of us searching to understand the voice of God, we must diligently and faithfully be committed to being more spiritual. This involves taking time to pray and study scripture, which helps us to develop the capacity to discern the voice of God. Let's take a look at the three components that make up the first principle of the Model of Faith, God Speaks.

God Speaks: The Voice of God

Abraham, Samuel, and Jesus are three examples depicting the first component of God Speaks, the Voice of God. Three passages of the Bible can be used to help us understand the way God communicates.

First, Genesis 12 tells the story of Abraham's calling. Genesis 12:1 says, "Now the Lord said to Abram, 'Go from your country and your kindred and your father's house to the land that I will show you.'" It is clear in the text that Abraham, whose name was Abram at the time, somehow discerned the voice of God. He either heard God speak to him the same way Sarah spoke to him or he understood God's voice from within his heart.

Although it is not clear what vehicle God used to communicate with Abraham, it is certain that Abraham understood that an invisible God was speaking. The Lord had a way to communicate with his servant, and Abraham had to understand that he was hearing and listening to the voice of God. God wants to communicate with all of his children. He wants to speak to us so we can follow his instructions. When we listen to and obey the voice of God, it leads to God's blessings. In Genesis 12, God told Abraham that he would be blessed, his name would be great, and he would be a blessing to others.

This is a major passage, not only because God was going to use a man who would become the father of many nations, but even greater, it would be through Abraham's family line that the Savior of the world would be born. Abraham's story is truly a story of a man who walked by faith. Genesis 12:1–3 is about Abraham listening to the voice of God. He not only listened but listened with a mind to obey. This is indicated in Genesis 26:5, where God said, "Abraham obeyed my voice and kept my charge, my commandments, my statutes, and my laws."

The second passage that helps us to understand the voice of God is found in 1 Samuel 3. This chapter tells us that when the prophet Samuel was a boy working with the priest Eli in the temple, he heard someone call his name. He thought Eli called him, so he ran to him.

However, it was not Eli who had called him. At the time, Samuel did not recognize the voice of God. Yet he would soon understand when the Lord was speaking to him. The scripture seems to indicate that God spoke to Samuel through spoken communication, like a man would speak to another man. The Lord may choose this direct means of communication with us today.

Are you listening for God to speak to you? Are you developing your ability to clearly listen to God? Like Samuel, there may be times when you need to seek guidance from someone who can help you understand what God is saying. Eli told Samuel, "Go, lie down, and if he calls you, you shall say, 'Speak, Lord, for your servant hears'" (1 Samuel 3:9).

We all need help at times discerning God's voice. If you know someone who is spiritually mature and has proven it through his or her personal experience to be in good fellowship with God, take time to talk with them. This person may be able to help you understand the message God may be saying to you. God may not choose to speak to you in an audible way. However, if you're striving to hear God's voice, understand that he wants to communicate to you.

The third example of God's voice is found in Jesus himself. Jesus was the voice of God because he was God in the flesh and spoke the words of the Father. He was perfect in communicating what the Father wanted to communicate to man. He never used the wrong words, misspoke, and injected his will over that of the Father's. God the Father validated the Son's words at the transfiguration. "This is my beloved Son, with whom I am well pleased; listen to him" (Matthew 17:5).

All during the ministry of Jesus, the twelve disciples learned that Jesus's words were the voice of God. The miracle of the feeding of the five thousand is an example of the power of Jesus's spoken words. All four gospels record this miracle. Jesus commanded the people to sit down, and after he gave thanks for the two fish and five loaves, he gave it to his disciples to feed the multitude of people. As a result, more than five thousand people were fed.

God Speaks: The Bible

The second component of God Speaks is the Bible, or scripture. The Bible is the written form by which we learn what God says. In Exodus 34:27, God instructs Moses, "Write these words, for in accordance with these words I have made a covenant with you and with Israel."

God not only told Moses, Joshua, and the apostle John (just to name a few) to write down his commandments and his laws but also, in essence, to record his will. We have knowledge of what God said because men of God wrote scripture as they were led by the guidance of the Holy Spirit (2 Peter 1:21).

God speaks to us through scripture. Reading and studying God's Word is very important for Christians. If the believer does not know scripture, he is like a soldier who is in the enemy's territory and does not know what commands his general has given. He's trying to go it alone and will possibly fail because he has not communicated with headquarters. The Bible is the voice of God, simply because its content is the written words of God. It is important to understand that Jesus used scripture to defeat Satan in the wilderness.

Each time Satan tempted Jesus, he countered with Old Testament scripture. This is depicted in Matthew 4, where Jesus used scripture from Deuteronomy 8:3, Deuteronomy 6:16, Deuteronomy 6:13, and Deuteronomy 10:20 to defeat Satan. He used scripture in its proper context to give Satan a severe blow at the beginning of his ministry. Jesus has given every believer an example to follow. He wants us to study scripture, to know what he has said in both the Old and New Testaments, and to use that knowledge to defeat our enemy.

One year during our church's Bible class, I challenged the students to learn more scriptures. I asked them to write down five new verses and review them each day during the week, as a way to help memorize them. The goal was to get more spiritual food into them by memorizing new scripture.

During subsequent Bible classes, I had them quote the scriptures that they had learned. I commended them for knowing most of the verses, even if they did not know them verbatim. Additionally I shared with the class the importance of getting, living, and giving ("G-L-G-ing") the Word. We must *get* the Word, *live* the Word, and then *give* the Word. I shared with the class that God wants us to study his Word (2 Timothy 2:15), be doers of his Word, (James 1:22) and share the Word with others (Matthew 28:19). For this to happen, we must begin by reading the Bible. Are you learning more scripture? Every Christian increases his or her ability to walk in God's will as they learn and apply more scriptures to their life.

God Speaks: The Role of Obedience

Finally, the third component of God Speaks is Obedience. Every believer must have a desire to obey God. As children of God, we should want to obey our heavenly Father. When God speaks to Christians, they should have a joyful heart to obey his voice. In Luke 1, the angel Gabriel told Mary that she was going to have a son.

Although she was unsure how she could have a child (since she was a virgin), she stated, "Let it be to me according to your word" (Luke 1:38). She was convinced that it was going to happen and was willing to do her part. She had a willing spirit of obedience even before she had an opportunity to obey.

We as Christians must have a "let it be" spirit within us. We must be willing to let God's will be done by our willingness to obey his every command. In Isaiah 6, the prophet Isaiah saw a glorious vision. He was convicted as he heard God say, "Whom shall I send, and who will go for us?"

Isaiah responded by saying, "Here I am! Send me" (Isaiah 6:8). Isaiah demonstrated a willingness to obey the Lord's voice to go.

Ruth is another example of a person who had the desire to do the right thing. When Naomi, Ruth's mother-in-law, tried to urge her to go back to her own family (following the death of Naomi's husband and sons), Ruth stated, "Do not urge me to leave you or to return from following you. For where you go I will go, and where you lodge I will lodge. Your people shall be my people, and your God my God" (Ruth 1:16). Her mind was made up to stay with her mother-in-law at all cost.

Sunday after Sunday, many Christians go to church and listen to the minister preach the Word of God. Yet so many fail to obey the message that they hear. They hear the Word but don't have the desire to obey the Word. It is important for every believer to obey God's Word. The apostle James wrote, "But be doers of the word, and not hearers only, deceiving yourselves" (James 1:22). In addition, John MacArthur stated in his book The Master's Plan for the Church, "An obedient person uncompromisingly does whatever God says to do. If God commands something, that's it—there's nothing to argue about. It's important to have God's Word in our hearts and minds so we know how to be obedient."[2]

Israel's success as a nation was fundamentally founded on the premise that they were to be obedient to the voice of God. They heard the voice of God through Moses. The Lord told Israel, "If you will diligently listen to the voice of the Lord your God, and do that which is right in his eyes, and give ear to his commandments and keep all his statutes, I will put none of the diseases on you that I put on the Egyptians, for I am the Lord, your healer" (Exodus 15:26).

Every believer should have a spirit of obedience. Edwin Louis Cole stated, "Obedience is an act of faith; disobedience is a result of unbelief."[3] Whether you hear God's voice from reading the Bible or hearing a sermon, have a willing spirit to obey what is conveyed to you. It is important to be willing to step out in the direction in which he tells you to go. When the child of God is freely willing to obey God's voice, it is only then that he or she is in a position to exercise operational faith.

Conclusion

In this chapter, I have explained the first principle in the Model of Faith, which is called "God's Speaks." Understanding when God is speaking is the first step in living a life of faith. The three components—God's Voice, Bible, and Obedience—are ways in which the Lord communicates to his followers.

Believers must connect every day with the Father in an effort to understand his will for our lives. Spend quality time learning the various

---

[2] John MacArthur, *The Master's Plan for the Church*, (Chicago: The Moody Bible Institute of Chicago, 2008) 30.

[3] Edwin Louis Cole

ways God speaks to you, and then have a heart to be obedient to his every command. When we recognize the Lord's voice, then we can utilize our operational faith to accomplish his will. In the next chapter, I will discuss what operational faith is and how we are to use it.

Discussion Questions/Exercises

1. Does God communicate with you? In what ways? List three ways that you can improve your ability to discern the voice of God.

2. Begin to increase the number of Bible verses that you know. Write three to five new verses on an index card, or use some other method to record verses so you can practice memorizing them. Then ask someone to quiz you on them.

3. Understand that God wants you to obey his Word. Write down three areas of your life where you want to be more obedient to God. Write down the steps that you will take to help you obey his Word.

CHAPTER 3

Operational Faith

So faith comes from hearing, and hearing through the word of Christ.

—Romans 10:17

God's will for every person is for them to receive salvation. The apostle Paul wrote to his spiritual son Timothy, "This is good, and it is pleasing in the sight of God our Savior, who desires all people to be saved and to come to the knowledge of the truth" (1 Timothy 2:3–4).

Before a person can utilize operational faith, he or she must first have saving faith. They must repent of their sins and then confess Jesus as their personal Savior. Paul writes in Romans 10:9, "If you confess with your mouth that Jesus is Lord and believe in your heart that God raised him from the dead, you will be saved."

A person is saved based simply on God's grace and his or her confession of a hope in Christ. Ephesians 2:8 says, "For by grace you have been saved through faith. And this is not your own doing; it is the gift of God." Having faith is when a person expresses his or her belief in Jesus Christ. When anyone accepts Jesus as their personal Savior, he or she has been saved by faith. The person's belief gives them eternal life because they have opened their heart to accept the Savior of the world. The next step for the believer is to learn how to live by faith, each and every day of their life.

Faith is an essential spiritual quality that all Christians must use and live by. The prophet Habakkuk stated, "But the righteous shall live by his faith" (Habakkuk 2:4). The theologian Martin Luther stated, "God our Father has made all things depend on faith so that whoever has faith will have everything, and whoever does not have faith will have nothing."[4]

Operational Faith

Operational faith is the process by which a Christian operates his or her life by the Word of God, "for we walk by faith, not by sight" (2 Corinthians 5:7). As Christians, God has called us to live a life of faith, which I call "operational faith." It is when Christians operate their lives daily according to the Word of God. It does not mean that someone is reading the Bible every minute of the hour or praying every second of the day.

However, it does mean that the child of God has developed a routine of praying and reading scripture on a regular basis. When Christians live by faith, they please God. The Hebrew writer stated, "Without faith it is impossible to please him, for whoever would draw near to God must believe that he exists and that he rewards those who seek him" (Hebrews 11:6).

Therefore when Christians demonstrate faith, they please God. Without it, they do not. Operational faith is the process by which a Christian allows scripture to direct his or her decisions and thereby his or her path. Years ago, I developed a wider or global meaning of operational faith. I saw it to mean faith, as the lens that Christians use to see their future. It gives them the ability to change their circumstances and is the vessel they use to complete God's destiny for their lives.

---

[4] Daniel Taddeo, *Notable Quotables:"3000 Quotations from A to Z"* (Florida: Creation House Press, 2003) 55.

Operational Faith in Action

Let us examine operational faith in scripture. In chapter 2, we discussed the story of Abraham written in Genesis 12. In verses 1–3, Abraham heard the voice of God. "So Abram went, as the Lord had told him, and Lot went with him. Abram was seventy-five years old when he departed from Haran" (Genesis 12:4).

This reveals that Abraham went as the Lord had told him and made plans to leave. He told his wife, his nephew Lot, and all of the servants to pack their bags and get all their belongings together because they were leaving Haran. In contemporary times, Abraham may have said to his family, "I don't have all the details of where we're going, but say good-bye to your friends and other family members because I'm not sure when or if we will be back."

When Abraham did all he had to do and left his country based on the voice of God, he utilized operational faith. Abraham heard the word of the Lord and obeyed it. His obedience to God's voice was a demonstration of his faith in God.

All Christians must learn to operate their lives in the same way as Abraham. We must walk in the direction that God has told us to go. You should not think that you are incapable of doing such a drastic thing. God does not change, and you are just as important to God as Abraham was. God has a mission for your life, and it is important that you discover what it is by using your operational faith.

For some Christians, this may seem like a scary process, to go where you don't know, and all that you have is trust in God's Word. It is normal for people to utilize their knowledge, intelligence, and experience to propel them forward so they can achieve their goals. However, as Christians, we have not been called to be sight creatures. We are not dependent upon what we see, hear, and know. We have been called to walk after the Spirit.

Paul writes in Romans 8:4, "Who walk not according to the flesh but according to the Spirit." As Christians, we must learn how to relax in not knowing (understanding) what God is doing next. Our focus must be on what God has said or what scripture has revealed to us. We must develop a pattern of relying on the one on whom our faith is dependent.

The more we understand God's Word and the more we pray in the Spirit, our relationship with God gets stronger. This allows us to develop a spirit of discernment to recognize the voice of God. We can then internally comprehend when the Lord is speaking to us and subsequently understand that his voice must be obeyed.

Another example of obedience can be found in Joshua 6. The Lord instructed Joshua on how to defeat the people living in the city of Jericho. The Lord told him,

> You shall march around the city, all the men of war going around the city once. Thus, shall you do for six days. Seven priests shall bear seven trumpets of rams' horns before the ark. On the seventh day you shall march around the city seven times, and the priests shall blow the trumpets. (Joshua 6:3–4).

The Lord wanted Joshua and the children of Israel to defeat their enemy by using a faith walk. Joshua utilized his operational faith by obeying the words of the Lord. As a result, the walls of Jericho came down, and the children of Israel were victorious in defeating their enemy. We too must learn how to operate our lives by faith, daily submitting to God's Word.

Operational faith is all about doing what God has said. Our faith increases because we hear the Word of God. Paul states in Romans 10:17, "So faith comes from hearing, and hearing through the word of Christ." Christians must seriously take time to hear the Word of God. Hearing the Word preached and taught regularly has a profound impact on a person's faith. Along with hearing the Word, it is important to read and study the Bible, allowing the passages to become a part of who you are. The words of Christ should be part of your DNA.

Another example of operational faith is found in Matthew 8, which tells the story of the Roman centurion who had a servant who was ill. The centurion locates Jesus and asks him to heal his servant. As Jesus is about to go home with him, the centurion states that he is not worthy to have Jesus come to his home. So he asks Jesus to just speak the word and his servant would be healed. The Roman centurion had faith that Jesus could heal his servant, on the strength of his word alone.

Scripture tells us that Jesus was amazed at the centurion's faith. "Truly, I tell you, with no one in Israel have I found such faith" (Matthew 8:10). He was right, and Jesus commended him for such faith. Every Christian should desire Jesus to say the same about his or her level of faith. When Christians use their operational faith, it not only means that they are obeying the voice of God, but it also means that they can speak the Word with confidence to situations in their lives and believe that the will of God will be done.

Every believer must understand that there is power in the spoken Word. When Peter and John were making their way to the temple to pray (Acts 3), a lame man asked them for money. Peter looked at the man and told him that he did not have any money. But instead he said to him, "What I do have I give to you. In the name of Jesus Christ of Nazareth, rise up and walk! And he took him by the right hand and raised him up" (Acts 3:6–7). Peter spoke to the man in Jesus's name and then helped him get off his mat.

Both Peter and John believed that their faith was capable of healing the man. They used the power that faith commands. What faith Peter, John, and the Roman centurion demonstrated! Peter and John believed that they could heal the lame man; the Roman centurion believed that Jesus's word alone had power to heal.

When you operate by faith, you can speak the Word to your various circumstances. No matter what the situation is—poor health, layoff notice, crises in your family, or some other situation—ask yourself the following questions: What Bible verse is relevant to my circumstance?

How can I stand on God's Word in this situation? What am I doing to develop my faith?

Attending worship service, Bible class, Sunday school, and other small groups that focus on studying God's Word are productive ways that Christians can gain biblical knowledge that will grow their faith. Try your best to attend your church's Bible study or seek out a Bible class that you can attend. Equally as important as going to Bible class is your faithful attendance in Bible class.

Many Christians don't understand that their irregular attendance in Bible class affects their spiritual growth. Just like we need healthy and regular diet to grow physically and mentally, the child of God needs a consistent spiritual feeding on the Word of God. Bible scholar John Butler says, "Our study of the Scriptures must be continuous. We will not learn everything the first time we inquire of the Scriptures. God does not reveal everything to us on our first show of interests. We must pursue again and again before we learn many truths."[5]

The statement "Our study of Scriptures must be continuous" is very true. I often share with my adult Sunday school class that we never graduate from being a student of God's Word because there is so much to learn and not enough time in life to learn it all.

Faith Commands Power

When we truly operate our lives by operational faith, we can command change to occur. Faith has the ability to change life's situations. Having strong faith exemplifies your understanding that all things are possible because God can do all things. Jesus stated to his disciples, "If you have faith like a grain of mustard seed, you will say to this mountain, 'Move from here to there,' and it will move, and nothing will be impossible for you" (Matthew 17:20).

---

[5] John G. Butler, *Jesus Christ His Incarnation* (LBC Publications, 2000) 258.

Some Bible scholars believe that Jesus was speaking figuratively and not literally. Was he only speaking figuratively? Can we believe that God can, if it is his will, give us the ability to move a real mountain? Did he divide the real Red Sea when Moses raised his hand over it? We must not lose sight of the fact that operational faith commands power, power to bring about real change.

I've always enjoyed reading the story of Jesus cursing the fig tree during his last week in ministry. The Word of God tells us that Jesus saw a fig tree and cursed it because it did not have any fruit on it. The next day as they were passing through the same area, the disciples saw that the fig tree was dead. Jesus told his disciples, "If you have faith and do not doubt, you will not only do what has been done to the fig tree, but even if you say to this mountain, 'Be taken up and thrown into the sea,' it will happen. And whatever you ask in prayer, you will receive, if you have faith" (Matthew 21:21–22).

It is important to remember that Jesus's disciples were ordinary men who had plenty of faults and made mistakes. They were people just like us. They were not fictitious superheroes. However, Jesus said to them in so many words, if they use their operational faith and do not doubt, they can command the *its* in life. What are the *its*? They are objects or things that we encounter.

Here are a few examples in the Bible of men using operational faith to command the *its*:

- Moses speaking to the rock and water coming out
- Joshua commanding the sun and the moon to be still
- Elisha taking a tree branch and using it to cause iron to float on water
- The disciples of Christ (following the words of Christ) taking two fish and five loaves of bread and feeding more than five thousand people

Christians today may not understand how faith can be actualized in their own personal situations. One way that operational faith can be used is to open your house door when you left your keys inside the house or commanding your car to start after it has stopped because you think you're out of gas. All things are possible if our faith develops/grows to the size of a mustard seed.

Utilizing operational faith means that all situations and life experiences are subject to our faith. My own experience took place a few years ago when my wife and I were returning home from Memphis, Tennessee. We went to Memphis to attend a church conference. While I was driving on the highway several hours away from home, it started pouring down rain. In the past when a similar situation occurred, my first reaction was to pray. However, this time I felt the Spirit saying to me to use my faith.

This was one of the first times that I became aware of the difference between my praying to God and my having faith in God. The Spirit said to speak to the storm and to tell the rain to stop raining. It was raining so hard that I could barely see the cars in front of me, but I obeyed the Spirit. Many Christians may not have thought to speak to the rain when they could barely see the cars in front of them. They may have chosen the commonsense approach, to slow down and pull over. This may be the practical solution because the power to bring about change is based on an individual's faith level.

Everyone in Jesus's day did not have faith like the Roman centurion, who asked Jesus to just speak the word and his servant would be healed. In my situation, I understood that I should use my faith in this situation and say to the storm "stop raining." I said it with confidence, and minutes later, the rain eased up and eventually stopped.

Later it started raining again, but my faith in God was greatly increased on this trip. I am not saying for you to do the same thing in a similar situation, but I am saying to work on increasing your faith. I am saying, if you utilize your operational faith, change can occur. On this occasion,

I clearly understood that the Spirit was not telling me to pray but to use operational faith.

Additionally I understood the will of God. We were on a trip to support others in the ministry. As a result, if God sent us to support them, he would provide for us and return us safely home. This experience helped me to stand on the Word of God through a real storm. I found the Hebrew writer's words to be true. He would never leave us nor forsake us (Hebrews 13:5b).

Faith and Trust

Along with our ability to use operational faith, every believer must understand that he or she must trust God as he or she moves forward by faith. Trusting God to provide for us and to direct our path strengthens our faith. Trusting God is the padding that protects our faith. When a football player plays in a game, he must have on his uniform. Underneath his uniform he wears shoulder pads, rib pads, and thigh and knee pads to protect him when he comes into contact with opposing players.

When we trust God, it is the padding to our faith. Trusting God undergirds operational faith. When we trust God, we rely on God to work out our situation, even when we do not understand how he is going to do it. Trust walks with faith, just like two friends walking together in the park.

When we trust God, we remember what God has already done, and because he's God, we know he can do it again. When we think in this manner, operational faith is empowered to move forward because we're trusting God. A good example is found in the book of Daniel concerning the three Hebrew boys.

Their trust in God led them to stand on the convictions of their faith. Their minds were made up that they were not going to bow and worship the king's golden idol. They knew the true and living God, and they knew his word, "You shall have no other gods before me … You shall not bow down to them or serve them" (Exodus 20:3,5). Therefore, they could trust God to deliver them from the fiery furnace or deliver them from this sinful world. They had faith in God and totally trusted him. They knew the Word of God. So they spoke to the king in faith and said,

> If this be so, our God whom we serve is able to deliver us from the burning fiery furnace, and he will deliver us out of your hand, O king. But if not, be it known to you, O king, that we will not serve your gods or worship the golden image that you have set up. (Daniel 3:17–18)

What powerful words from the three Hebrew boys! They trusted God to handle their situation even when they did not know how he was going to handle it. Maybe the Hebrew boys knew the psalmist's words, "In God I trust; I shall not be afraid. What can man do to me?" (Psalm 56:11).

In the situations that we face today, we must trust God to work them out. I remember many years ago when I worked for the government. My department received a bomb threat. The caller did not specify which office was going to be bombed. However, the threat was taken very seriously, and many of my coworkers were afraid to come to work.

As a precaution, a security guard was assigned at the entrance of the office building. During this experience, I asked myself, *Does my faith work in reality? Am I truly depending on God to protect me?* For many Christians, their faith remains attached to the pages of the Bible and not to their hearts. I had to remember Proverbs 3:5. "Trust in the Lord with all your heart, and do not lean on your own understanding."

I demonstrated my faith in this situation by continuing to come to work and trusting God to protect me no matter how much fear was around me. After several weeks, my employer determined that there was no longer a threat to the agency, and they removed the security guard.

Each and every day, Christians must walk by faith. At the same time, they must trust God as they encounter trials and tribulations. When you are faced with a tragedy, keep the faith by keeping God's Word in your heart.

Another great story of a man who kept trusting God while facing adversities was Job. Job could have forsaken God, or like his wife insisted, "Curse God and die" (Job 2:9). However, Job's faith was steadfast. His mind was made up, and he was determined to trust God. Is your mind made up that you will always and through all situations trust God?

Faith and Decisions

Lastly, every Christian must understand the correlation between decision making and faith. God's will is that his children make good decisions in life. For the Christian, good decisions can only come from what God's Word says. Effectively using operational faith is when we understand what God has said and then deciding to follow his instructions (scripture). Faith helps us implement the decisions that pleases God.

In Luke 10:42, Jesus commended Mary for choosing to listen to him instead of doing household tasks. Mary decided to sit at the feet of Jesus and listen to him teach. However, she could have decided to help her sister, Martha, with being busy around the house. Another example of how your faith impacts your decisions is found in the book of Exodus concerning the midwives.

The midwives were told by Pharaoh, when they assist the Hebrew women who give birth, to deliver the girl infants but to kill the boys. The midwives made a decision not to obey Pharaoh's command. They used their operational faith to save the male infants. They made a conscious decision to have faith because they reverenced God.

The scripture says, "But the midwives feared God and did not do as the king of Egypt commanded them, but let the male children live" (Exodus 1:17). The midwives' wise decisions led to God blessing them. Scripture says, "So God dealt well with the midwives. And the people multiplied and grew very strong. And because the midwives feared God, he gave them families" (Exodus 1:20–21).

How are you making your decisions? Are you seeking God's will? How are you deciding where you want to work? How are you deciding whether to buy a house or rent an apartment? How are you making your decision to get married or stay single? The first step in making good decisions is to ask God to help you make the right decisions. Seeking God in prayer is an important step in making the right decision. Proverbs 3:6 says, "In all your ways acknowledge him, and he will make straight your paths."

I will discuss prayer more in depth in the next chapter. However, after you have prayed and have an understanding as to what God has said, the next step is to step out on your faith. God may use someone in your life who has wisdom, or he may choose to reveal it to you another way. Whatever way he chooses, it will be in line with his Word. God's Word gives you answers to life's situations. If you know his Word, you can then use operational faith by making your decision based on what God's Word has revealed.

Conclusion

I have discussed two of the four major principles in the Model of Faith: God Speaks and Operational Faith. God Speaks simply means "What is God saying through the voice of God and scripture?" Operational Faith means "doing what God says."

Every Christian should live his or her life hearing the voice of God and then obeying it. Before Adam and Eve disobeyed God in the garden of Eden, their life was all about hearing God's voice and doing what he said. When they sinned, their relationship with God changed, creating a need for them and subsequently everyone else to learn how to operate their lives by faith.

Discussion Questions/Exercises

1. Name three ways you are going to increase your operational faith. Create a plan that shows the things you are doing to lead to a stronger faith.

2. Identify seven scriptures that you can quote that will help you use operational faith in five different circumstances (This will help you learn to speak the Word when dealing with situations that develop in your life.)

3. Research the Bible and write down three examples of individuals commanding the *its* or *things* to obey them. What does this teach you about the power of faith?

Chapter 4

The Power of Prayer

The prayer of a righteous person has great power as it is working.

—James 5:16

It is important for all Christians to have quiet time with God, as previously stated in chapter 2. Each day I strive to have QTD to activate my operational faith. I have learned that spiritual power comes as a result of consistent and constant prayer time with the Lord. Every believer must make it mandatory to communicate daily with God. What does your prayer time look like? Are you praying after you wake up in the morning? Are you praying during your lunch? Is your prayer time basically done at night before you go to sleep, or have you learned to pray throughout the day?

If your goal is to obtain a powerful faith that will lead you into your destiny, then you must understand the importance of developing a strong prayer life. We must remember that the apostle Paul said, "Pray without ceasing" (1 Thessalonians 5:17).

Prayer is more than simple words we say to God. It must be sincere heartfelt utterances that we express to God. God knows our hearts as well as what's on our minds, so he desires communication that is filled with truth and sincerity. As a result, when we call on God via spoken communication or silently (within our heart), we must always remember to do it honestly.

We must remember that prayer is a child of God speaking directly to his or her heavenly Father. If operational faith is putting into motion the very words of God, then prayer is a Christian's heartfelt communication to an invisible and all-hearing God. Do you remember Hannah's prayer in 1 Samuel 1? She prayed sincerely for a child. She cried out to God and prayed until she even got the priest Eli's attention. God heard her prayer and blessed her.

Believing Your Prayer

When you pray, do you believe God hears your prayer? There was a time when I questioned whether God heard my prayers. It was hard for me to see evidence of God answering my prayers. However, one day I was reading John 11 and stumbled across verse 42. "I knew that you always hear me, but I said this on account of the people standing around, that they may believe that you sent me."

These are Jesus's words that he prayed to the Father. When I read the words "I knew that you always hear me," I realized at that moment that the Father always hears his children's prayer when they sincerely pray to him. He hears me. He listens to me. I really know that he does. These words seemed to stick with me. I believed them. Now I believe God hears me just like I believe my wife hears me when I'm speaking two feet from her.

You must remove all doubt from your prayers and believe that God is listening to every word you say. God does hear us! He may not give you the answer that you expect or answer your prayer according to your will, but you must trust him to do what is best for you. Keep on believing that God hears you and remember Psalm 77:1, "I cry aloud to God, aloud to God, and he will hear me."

Prayer and Listening

As you develop a pattern of praying consistently, it is important to understand that you must develop the skill of listening to God in prayer. Prayer is a Christian's way of talking with God, but we must understand that God can also speak to our hearts as we pray. The art of listening to God must be developed. We listen to God by pausing in prayer. As we pray, we are thanking God, confessing our sins, interceding for others, and asking God to grant our petitions, but in addition we must leave time to listen for his voice. Often our prayers are filled with what we want God to do for us, without giving considerable attention to the will of God. So as you pray, create time to pause in your prayer expecting God, if he chooses, to speak to you.

The prophet Daniel was a man of great faith and prayer. Daniel prayed fervently for his people. While he was praying, God sent an angel to him. Daniel wrote,

> While I was speaking and praying, confessing my sin and the sin of my people Israel, and presenting my plea before the Lord my God for the holy hill of my God, while I was speaking in prayer, the man Gabriel, whom I had seen in the vision at the first, came to me in swift flight at the time of the evening sacrifice. He made me understand, speaking with me and saying, "O Daniel, I have now come out to give you insight and understanding." (Daniel 9:20–22)

Daniel received a message from the Lord as he was praying. We too must realize that God can give us a message during our prayer time with him.

If you are in the habit of saying your prayers and then quickly going about your daily routine, you will miss the opportunity of discovering a deeper level of praying. We cannot rush God in prayer. He speaks to us on his own timetable. Our role is to allow time to listen during our prayers.

Also realize that the Spirit, while we are listening in prayer, may choose to speak to us by revealing the Word of God to us. The Spirit may tell a minister which verse to preach in the coming weeks or give a wife a passage on trusting God as she deals with a challenging situation with her husband.

Listening to God in prayer is a powerful tool that you can develop as you learn to devote more time to pray. The skill of listening in prayer helps to develop your operational faith because praying helps you discern the voice of God. Operational faith is all about obeying the voice of God. To do this, the believer needs to have a clear understanding when God is speaking and what he is saying. Listening in prayer creates a bridge for the child of God to operate effectively by faith.

Prayer and Operational Faith Working Independently

Prayer and operational faith are two spiritual principles that every Christian should utilize on a continuous basis. The Bible has numerous scriptures on faith and prayer. Many scriptures support both spiritual principles. "And the prayer of faith will save the one who is sick, and the Lord will raise him up. And if he has committed sins, he will be forgiven" (James 5:15).

As a child of God, I want to exercise operational faith every day, but I also know that I must remain in contact with God through prayer. During my personal devotion, near the end of my prayer time, I ask God to allow me to utilize my operational faith. I realize that I need God to speak to me through scripture (his voice), and as I understand what he is saying, I must then step out in that direction.

Faith and prayer work together, but it also is important to understand that faith can operate independently of prayer. Faith operates based on the Word of God or the voice of God. In Mark 11, Jesus was preparing to enter Jerusalem. He gave instructions to two of his disciples to go into a nearby town and bring to him a donkey that had never been ridden on. He also gave the disciples instructions on what to say if anyone asked why they were taking the animal.

The disciples obeyed Jesus's words. They operated by faith. They found the animal, as Jesus had said, and explained the reason why they were taking it. On another occasion, Jesus instructed Peter to go to the sea and catch a fish. In the fish's mouth would be a coin, sufficient enough to pay the taxes owed to the government.

Peter obeyed the words of Jesus and was able to pay the necessary taxes. In both situations, the disciples used operational faith. The disciples did not have to pray to God because they understood the voice of Jesus, and because they believed Jesus, they obeyed his words. How do we use operational faith independent of prayer? When a situation arises that you must make a decision about and you know from reading and studying God's Word what it says, you don't have to ask God (pray) what is his will when his Word has already revealed his will to you. You can pray but understand God has already spoken through his written Word. Christians are to make their decisions based on what the Bible says, and when you have done this, you have used operational faith independent of prayer.

There are times when we seem to have only prayer. We don't understand how to use operational faith. Several years ago, I took a flight from Chicago to Denver on my way to a conference. All during the flight, the turbulence was strong. The captain kept on the "fasten seat belt" sign throughout most of the flight. All I could do was pray, or so I thought. I prayed through the physical reality of my fear. Now as I look back on the experience, I wondered where my faith was. It seemed nowhere to be found. Yet I did not forget how to pray. Prayer was my company keeper and companion during that flight.

When we are not certain of our next step forward, we must pray to get further directions. When your faith seems to have hit a wall or mountain and it seems like you've come to a point where you don't know what to do next, then you must cry out to God in prayer so he can direct your path. In that instance, prayer is like a backup quarterback who enters the game when the starter, faith, goes down.

If you can recall when Jesus and his disciples were on the ship and the storm arose, the disciples decided that they needed to wake up Jesus. Mark 4:38–40 says,

> But he was in the stern, asleep on the cushion. And they woke him and said to him, "Teacher, do you not care that we are perishing?" And he awoke and rebuked the wind and said to the sea, "Peace! Be still!" And the wind ceased, and there was a great calm. He said to them, "Why are you so afraid? Have you still no faith?"

The disciples of Christ should have used their faith to either quiet the storm or relax knowing that Jesus was on the boat with them. However, because of their fear, they had to call on Jesus. I also had to pray while on the plane during the rough turbulence when I should have relaxed by trusting God's Word, knowing that he was with me during the flight. The Lord wants his children to always use operational faith in every situation that they face. Yet he also knows that at times they will need to pray when their faith becomes shaky or vulnerable to fear or attacks from the enemy.

Prayer Supporting Operational Faith

In the Old Testament, there are examples of individuals who used prayer to support their faith. Moses was a man that God used to lead the children of Israel out of Egypt. God told Moses to travel toward the Red Sea. As they were traveling in the direction that God told them to go, the Egyptian army pursued them. The children of Israel became afraid, and Moses cried out to God. Notice the Model of Faith in action.

First, Moses heard the voice of God instructing him to tell the children of Israel what to do (Exodus 12). They were to prepare the Passover meal, put blood on their doorposts, and then be dressed to leave Egypt. Second, the children of Israel obeyed Moses' voice by doing the things that he instructed them to do. They left Egypt based on Moses' instructions, which were based on his understanding of what God said to him. Approximately 2 million Israelites rejoiced as they were leaving

Egypt after being in slavery for 430 years. They were walking by faith and utilizing their operational faith.

As they traveled in the direction that God sent them, they discovered that the army of the Egyptians was following them. The children of Israel became afraid for their lives, and Moses prayed. The Israelites' faith was replaced with fear because of the approaching Egyptian army. As a result, they began to complain to Moses and cry out to God.

They no longer had faith in God or Moses. Moses tried to tell them not to worry about the Egyptians because God would take care of them. "The Lord said to Moses 'Why do you cry to me? Tell the people of Israel to go forward'" (Exodus 14:15). Moses' prayers led to God giving further instructions on what to do when trouble came their way.

Years ago when I would drive downtown to work, I would look for a spot to park my car. I often prayed and asked God to lead me to an open parking space. Although sometimes I would have to drive around for several minutes, I would not give up.

One day as I was nearing my office building, a car came right out, and I was able to drive right in. I knew it wasn't a coincidence or luck, but God answering prayer by my ability to use operational faith. Jesus answered my prayer according to his Word in Matthew 21:22, "And whatever you ask in prayer, you will receive, if you have faith."

Prayer and Fasting

To gain a powerful prayer life, Christians must practice the discipline of fasting. Fasting helps to strengthen a believer's relationship with God. Prayer and fasting provides believers with a closer intimacy with God. Many of God's servants prayed and fasted for spiritual breakthroughs and subsequently received God's blessings. Among them were Nehemiah, Daniel, Paul, and Esther. These saints, along with others, prayed and fasted with great success. Jesus gave his disciples instructions on how to fast.

> And when you fast, do not look gloomy like the hypocrites … But when you fast, anoint your head and wash your face, that your fasting may not be seen by others but by your Father who is in secret. And your Father who sees in secret will reward you. (Matthew 6:16–18)

Fasting that is done in secret gets God's attention. Fasting takes the believer's attention away from physical concerns and allows him or her to have a greater dependency on spiritual things. Fasting enables prayer to become more spiritual. Prayer and fasting impact operational faith by developing the believer's ability to discern God's voice. In the book *Fasting* by Jentezen Franklin, the author states, "Fasting makes you more sensitive to the timing and voice of the Holy Spirit."[6] He also writes, "Fasting prepares the way for God to give you fresh revelation, fresh vision, and clear purpose."[7]

There are many Christians who have never fasted. They have not experienced a closer relationship with God that comes from prayer and fasting; nor have they experienced the power that is released as a result of fasting. When we pray and fast on a continuous basis, we not only develop a stronger prayer life, but a more powerful faith life as well. James 5:16 says, "The prayer of a righteous person has great power as it is working." The fervent prayer has the ability to heal because the believer truly believes that God can use them as a vessel to heal. The believer's prayer is connected to his or her faith, which commands change.

When I first started pastoring and would visit members of my church who were in the hospital, I was unsure whether God could use me to heal someone who was sick. I did not have a proper understanding of God's will, nor the power of prayer and faith.

However, since those earlier days in ministry, I have learned that God can do all things even when the doctors have given up on the patient. God can use me as his vessel to raise up the sick, if he so chooses. I now

---

[6] Jentezen Franklin, Fasting, (Lake Mary, FL: Charisma House, 2008), 104

[7] Ibid., 47.

walk in the hospital room with complete trust in God knowing that miracles can be done that day by faith. My faith has grown because of my willingness to invest more time in prayer and fasting.

My friend, I urge you to start fasting. You can start by fasting one day from 6:00 a.m. to 6:00 p.m. Pray every hour at the top of the hour, and find time during the fast to read God's Word. Also try to avoid going around people who are eating while you are fasting to limit the temptation to break your fast. Most importantly, remember to have a joyful attitude during your fast. Do not go through the day with your head down and a big sad face that draws attention to yourself. You are fasting unto God, not to win the sympathy of people.

Conclusion

As you increase your prayer time with God, your relationship with him will become more intimate. As a result, you will gain a powerful prayer life. As Christians, we need all the power we can get to fight Satan. He is an enemy that must be defeated by prayer, fasting, faith, and the Word of God. According to Jentezen, "Fasting is a tremendous weapon and a source of power in the life of a believer[8] … The devil knows fasting releases God's power."[9]

Our prayer and fasting strengthens operational faith. Near the end of Jesus's life, he faced arrest, trials, and persecution by the Jews, the high priest, the Roman solders, Herod, and Pilot. Yet before all of that took place, he went to the garden of Gethsemane. There, he prayed earnestly to the Father. Jesus's prayer strengthened his faith and gave him the determination to complete the Father's will. His faith was empowered by prayer, which allowed him to die on the cross for the sins of many. Jesus showed us in the garden of Gethsemane that prayer strengthens faith.

---

[8] Ibid., 49.

[9] Ibid., 52.

As you walk by faith, as you use your operational faith, remember to keep developing your relationship with God through prayer. You will need a strong, intimate prayer life as your faith accomplishes God's will. In addition to prayer supporting faith, the third principle in the Model of Faith, you will need to use the spiritual principle of patience with operational faith. In the next chapter, we will explain why patience is a spiritual principle that every Christian needs to possess.

Discussion Questions/Exercises

1. How often do you pray to God? Begin to increase your prayer time with God. If you are praying for ten minutes each day, increase it by five minutes. Increasing prayer time with God develops patience and strengthens your relationship with him. Develop a prayer chart or prayer diary to track how often you pray during the month.

2. Practice listening to God in prayer. If you pray for ten minutes, use three minutes to listen to God before you end your prayer. Try to do this for two weeks.

3. Schedule a day(s) you will fast. Write down how you will stay connected to God throughout the day. You can also state how often you will pray and read scripture.

CHAPTER 5

The Power of Patience

I waited patiently for the Lord; And he inclined unto me and heard my cry.

—Psalm 40:1

Patience represents the fourth principle in the model of faith. Patience is a spiritual virtue that all Christians must possess. Patience is being steadfast. It is waiting on God until he reveals what direction faith should take. Patience is connected to operational faith and prayer. When a child of God does not know which direction to walk by faith, he or she must pray to God. They must then wait on God to reveal his will. God cannot be rushed. His timetable is not the same as ours. Therefore, every Christian must patiently wait for God's instructions in all his or her decisions—big or small.

Patience is a godly quality that is difficult for many Christians to demonstrate in their lives. I would suggest that it is easier for a Christian to pray than to be patient. We often cry out to God, "Lord help me," but we lose patience when God does not act in the time frame that we expect. The main reason that Christians must be patient is because God is patient. His patience is demonstrated by his desire that all sinners be saved and not lost. If you are not saved today, God is patiently waiting for you to accept Jesus as your Savior.

Peter writes, "The Lord is not slow to fulfill his promise as some count slowness, but is patient toward you, not wishing that any should perish, but that all should reach repentance" (2 Peter 3:9).

As wicked as the world was in Genesis 6 during the time of Noah, God did not destroy the earth immediately. Rather he chose to allow Noah 120 years in which to build the ark. During the 120-year period, God was patient toward the people in that they could see Noah building the ark and have time to change their ways. Although Noah's family were the only ones saved on the ark, God's patience was shown during this generation.

Why Patience?

When I was a boy, I couldn't wait for my birthday or Christmas to come, as I was eager to see what gifts I would receive. One year, I wanted a new bicycle for Christmas, so I came down the stairs very early on Christmas morning to see if the bike was underneath the tree. I was so excited to find that it was there. As a child, I could hardly wait until the morning.

On many occasions during my teenage years, I anxiously awaited my birthdays. I wanted the cake, ice cream, and all the presents right away. However, as an adult, my birthdays seemed to come too quickly. Every time I look around, it seems as if another birthday is here. The same kind of mind-set that I have now concerning my birthday is what I'm learning to have when it comes to patiently waiting on God. I have learned that I cannot hurry God. Therefore, I must patiently trust him. God is a patient God, and all believers must learn to live patient lives.

Why should we show patience in our lives? It is because patience helps us to operate by faith. When we do not understand the next step to take by faith, patience says, "Wait on God to lead you." God knows when to act or how to direct our path. If we do not have patience connected to our faith, we will take matters into our own hands. This can cause us to make bad decisions. The Lord has given the spiritual gift of patience to Christians so they can relax in his will, knowing that he is still in control.

God also wants his believers to show patience with one another. Each believer must grow in faith and patience. Sometimes God uses life experiences to teach us how to become patient with each other. One day I went to the grocery store to purchase a few items. I had planned on this being a quick stop, so I grabbed the items and proceeded toward the checkout line designated for fifteen items or less. There were only two people in front of me, including the customer currently being waited on.

However, to my dismay, there was a problem with a coupon the person was trying to use. The cashier tried one thing after the other to get the register to accept the coupon, to no avail. Meanwhile, the person in front of me and myself were wondering what in the world was going on. However, we waited patiently.

What seemed to be a quick trip to the grocery store turned into an additional twenty minutes waiting in a line. My patience was tried to the fullest extent that day.

I wanted to shout out to the clerk, "Call your manager or do something to get this line moving again!"

Instead I waited "patiently" until the cashier resolved the situation. God not only wants us to wait on him, he also wants us to be patient with other people. He wants us to use faith in all situations and to show patience in situations that we cannot control.

Scripture reveals how God wants believers to show patience with others. Paul writes, "I therefore, a prisoner for the Lord, urge you to walk in a manner worthy of the calling to which you have been called, with all humility and gentleness, with patience, bearing with one another in love" (Ephesians 4:1–2).

Paul wanted Christians to have patience toward one another as well as to have other spiritual virtues. He also stated in 1 Corinthians 13:4,

"Love is patient and kind; love does not envy or boast; it is not arrogant." Paul knew that Jesus was the church's perfect example of demonstrating patience. He said to his spiritual son Timothy, "But I received mercy for this reason, that in me, as the foremost, Jesus Christ might display his perfect patience as an example to those who were to believe in him for eternal life" (1 Timothy 1:16).

Jesus showed patience with his disciples and the Pharisees and Scribes. His patience was illustrated in his being merciful and kind. His will was that all would repent and accept him as Savior. When the body of Christ wears the garment of patience, they please God, and their faith is made stronger.

Patience and Prayer

I've always viewed patience and prayer as two friends that support operational faith. Even when we have a strong prayer life, we must also have a spirit of patience. You may go through the routine of praying for something, but do you also go through the process of patience? As a pastor, members at times share with me that they made an important decision and indicate that they had prayed about it.

In one instance, I stated, "Yes, you have prayed about it, but have you waited about it?"

Though not grammatically correct, I was trying to let the member know that just because you prayed about it, that doesn't mean that God has told you to do it. Sometimes God says "wait." There are other times when we simply do not know what the Lord is saying. Oftentimes it seems like God's answer is delayed, but we must remember that he doesn't work on our timetable. God is always on time, and we cannot confine God to our time.

After we have prayed, we must be prepared to show patience, understanding that God knows the best time to answer our prayers. Some answers come immediately; others may take years. Regardless, all along the way we are trusting God that he will answer our prayer. Jesus illustrated the point of keeping the faith while praying in Luke 18 in the parable of the persistent widow.

In this parable, the widow was pleading with the judge for help concerning her situation. However, the judge did not answer her immediately. The widow continued to be persistent, and eventually it paid off. Scripture says, "I will give her justice, so that she will not beat me down by her continual coming" (Luke 18:5).

And Jesus went on to say to his disciples, "And will not God give justice to his elect, who cry to him day and night? Will he delay long over them? I tell you, he will give justice to them speedily. Nevertheless, when the Son of Man comes, will he find faith on earth?" (Luke 18:7–8).

This is an indication that we should learn to be patient with God after we pray. Keep believing that God will reveal your next step to you. He will direct you regarding which house to buy. He will reveal to you whether or not to relocate to another city. He knows how to place on your spirit whether or not you should marry the person that you are dating. As Christians, we must learn to become content as we patiently wait for the Lord to speak.

Patience and Operational Faith

The Old Testament gives examples of both men and women who exemplified great patience as well as great faith. As we examine Abraham's life again, we see that he showed patience as he waited on God to fulfill his promise to him. Hebrews 6:15 says, "And thus Abraham, having patiently waited, obtained the promise."

Abraham waited twenty-five years for Isaac, and although he had Ishmael fourteen years earlier, he was not the son of promise. God's son of promise, Isaac, was born by Abraham's wife, Sarah. Abraham was living by faith beginning from the time God called him and throughout the twenty-five-year period. He patiently waited for God to do what God promised that he would do.

We often use Job as an example when we talk about patience. Job gives us a good example of a man who waited for his prayers to be answered. "As an example of suffering and patience, brothers, take the prophets who spoke in the name of the Lord. Behold, we consider those blessed who remained steadfast. You have heard of the steadfastness of Job, and you have seen the purpose of the Lord, how the Lord is compassionate and merciful" (James 5:10–11).

King David is referred to as a man after God's own heart. David was also a man who showed great patience. On many occasions, David had an opportunity to take King Saul's life during the time when King Saul was trying to kill David. However, David did not want to harm God's anointed king. David waited for God to give him the kingdom. David could have used his free will to become king, but he chose to patiently wait on God's will to be done, to anoint him at the proper time.

These are just a few of God's servants that demonstrated patience as they lived by faith. Faith is the Christian spiritual eyes that allow them to move forward. Patience is the virtue that walks alongside a person's faith as a partner to help him or her develop the discipline of waiting on God.

The Power of Patience

As we live according to the will of God, we must learn to walk in the Lord's patience. We are to hold fast to the Word of God, or the voice of God, and travel in the direction that God has told us to go. Our patience is connected to our faith. We rely on it when we don't understand what direction to take. Having patience does not mean you should stop everything and stand still. It means that you are actively doing what you know to do until God gives you direction on what to do next.

In the example given previously in chapter 4, the children of Israel had to wait 430 years for God to deliver them from slavery. While they waited for their change to come, the Egyptians continued to oppress and persecute them. Yet Israel did not forget God. They remained committed to God by trusting and praying to him. When God called Moses, he told him, "I have surely seen the affliction of my people who are in Egypt and have heard their cry because of their taskmasters. I know their sufferings" (Exodus 3:7).

You may be working for an employer who doesn't know how to treat their employees. You may not have received a raise for many years. You may have cried out to God for change, and there seems to be no response. Keep holding on to God's Word as you patiently wait on him. The Lord knows your circumstances, and he has heard your prayer. The true power of patience is in your ability to persevere through difficult times.

Through your stress and your struggles, don't give up on God. At the right time, he will direct your path. Find encouragement in the apostle James' words, "Be patient, therefore, brothers, until the coming of the Lord. See how the farmer waits for the precious fruit of the earth, being patient about it, until it receives the early and the late rains. You also, be patient. Establish your hearts, for the coming of the Lord is at hand" (James 5:7–8).

Conclusion

Christians must live patient lives because patience strengthens our faith. We must understand that as we live a life of faith, our faith must be connected to the spiritual discipline of patience. Every believer must learn how to wait on the Lord. We must wait patiently on the Lord to give us direction on how to proceed. As Christians, we must also show great patience with one another. As believers, we continually increase our patience by adhering to other spiritual virtues that will help us grow in patience.

The apostle Peter writes in 2 Peter 1:5–7, "For this very reason, make every effort to supplement your faith with virtue, and virtue with knowledge, and knowledge with self-control, and self-control with steadfastness, and steadfastness with godliness, and godliness with brotherly affection, and brotherly affection with love." As we operate our lives by faith, we must remember to utilize patience to help us as we seek to discover the will of God for our lives.

Discussion Questions/Exercises

1. Which person in the Bible can you use as an example to follow in exemplifying patience? Research his or her life story and try to learn what made him or her have patience.

2. During a two-week period, write down at least three instances when you had to show patience to others. Evaluate yourself on your attitude and actions during these times. What were you thinking and doing that helped or hindered you in being patient? Are there any biblical verses that can help you improve your ability to be patient the next time a similar situation arises?

3. How does patience support your faith? Do you see patience as a means to use your faith to please God? If so, in what way?

Part II

Utilizing Operational Faith in Your Life

Chapter 6

Enemies of Operational Faith

Fight the good fight of the faith.

—1 Timothy 6:12a

America has many enemies. Some of them are ISIS, Iran, Russia, and North Korea. America must always be prepared to defend itself against her enemies. Like America, the Christian church has a spiritual enemy called Satan. Every day Satan tries to attack and defeat Christians. He tries to destroy their faith and make them denounce their love for God. However, God has equipped his church with fighting power and has given her spiritual armor to crush Satan and his demons. Operational faith is one of the key spiritual weapons that a child of God must use to fight our spiritual enemies.

The apostle Paul encouraged the church to dress themselves in God's spiritual armor to fight the enemy. He wrote to the Ephesian church, "Put on the whole armor of God, that you may be able to stand against the schemes of the devil" (Ephesians 6:11). He further stated, "In all circumstances take up the shield of faith, with which you can extinguish all the flaming darts of the evil one" (Ephesians 6:16). Satan uses many methods to try to defeat Christians' faith.

One method is to attack Christians by using weaknesses of the flesh, which I call enemies of our faith. Satan's goal is to crush our faith and to stop us from serving God. He wants Christians to abandon the relationship that they have with God. Among the many enemies of our faith are unbelief, fear, complaining, worrying, pride, and lust. Before I discuss the enemies that affect our faith, let me discuss the importance of Christians having fighting power.

In the movie *We Were Soldiers* starring Mel Gibson, he played the role of an army colonel. Near the end of the movie, there is a scene where Mel Gibson's troops are losing the battle. The enemy is attacking from all sides and attempting to overrun the American troops. During a raging battle, the colonel stands up, not fearing for his life, looks around, and says to one of his men who has a radio the code word, "broken arrow."

The code is an emergency call to headquarters. It summons all American aircraft wherever they are to go to the aid of the battalion that is in jeopardy of being overtaken. The movie shows several American aircraft coming from everywhere to aid the American colonel and his men. They save the day and defeat the enemy.

When I think about this scene, I think about how Satan is fiercely fighting the children of God, how he is trying to defeat God's church with problems, pain, suffering, disappointments, trials, and other various adversities. One way the church can survive is by sending a spiritual SOS to heaven, asking the Father to come to the church's rescue and to empower her with fighting power to overcome all the schemes of the devil.

Every child of God must have fighting power. Having fighting power means that Christians have a spirit of wanting to defeat sin, Satan, and self. We must not want to give in to temptation or listen to Satan, as Eve listened to the serpent. We must follow what God has told us to do rather than what we "feel" that we want to do.

It is important that we realize that we can and will win the spiritual battle that we're up against. James writes, "Submit yourselves therefore to God. Resist the devil, and he will flee from you" (James 4:7). Fighting power is resisting power. When David fought Goliath, he not only had courage, but he had a willing spirit to fight. 1 Samuel 17:32 says, "David said to Saul, 'Let no man's heart fail because of him. Your servant will go and fight with this Philistine.'"

Peter also had fighting power. Although the Lord told Peter that he would deny him three times, it wasn't something that Peter wanted to do. He was willing to fight physically for Christ. He showed this when he struck the high priest's servant with his sword and cut off his right ear (John 18:10).

We need to understand that the enemy we face is real. He does not like you. You cannot be his friend. Peter likens Satan to a lion that goes around searching for those whom he can destroy (1 Peter 5:8). Peter goes on to say, "Resist him, firm in your faith" (1 Peter 5:9a). As we fight the enemies of our faith, we fight with the knowledge of knowing that we can defeat them. We fight knowing that we're on the winning side. We fight knowing that God's Word empowers our faith. It says, "Little children, you are from God and have overcome them, for he who is in you is greater than he who is in the world" (1 John 4:4). We fight knowing that the battle is the Lord's, and because of him, we will always be victorious.

Faith Fighting Unbelief

All Christians have a certain level of unbelief in them. You might not think that you have unbelief in you, but you do. Everyone is born with unbelief because no one automatically accepts Christ as his or her Savior the moment that they are born. Every person must discover Christ for himself or herself. That process usually begins with someone witnessing to them about Christ. All sinners must believe that Jesus Christ is the Savior of the world in order to receive salvation.

Paul and Silas responded to the Philippian jailor when he asked what he had to do to be saved. "Believe in the Lord Jesus, and you will be saved, you and your household" (Acts 16:31). Once you believe in Christ, you must continually feed your spirit on the Word of God in order to grow in Christ.

The apostle Paul said to Timothy, "Do your best to present yourself to God as one approved, a worker who has no need to be ashamed, rightly handling the word of truth" (2 Timothy 2:15).

What is unbelief? It is the absence of faith or not believing what God has said in his spoken or written Word. Christians must believe all of God's Word and that he can do all things. We must believe that God will do just what God's Word says he will do. The disciples of Christ spent three and a half years with the Lord, yet they still had plenty of unbelief even on the day of his resurrection.

When we believe God's Word, we live by his Word. We walk according to his Word by utilizing operational faith. So often Satan attacks a Christian's faith by having him or her doubt that God will do exactly what he said he would do. The apostle Thomas, one of the twelve disciples, has been known as "doubting Thomas."

When Christ rose from the dead, he appeared to ten of his disciples. However, Thomas was not present. Thomas expressed his unbelief to the other disciples by proclaiming, "Unless I see in his hands the mark of the nails and place my finger into the mark of the nails, and place my hand into his side, I will never believe" (John 20:25).

How do we as Christians defeat the enemy of unbelief? We must fight unbelief by praying, fasting, studying the Word, hearing the preaching of God's Word, and talking to other Christians who are walking close with God. Mature saints can help us understand how God has always been faithful. They can share with us how their faith in him has kept them through their various life experiences.

In Mark 9, the disciples of Christ could not heal a man's son who was possessed with a demon. When Jesus came down from the mountain, the man approached Christ and asked him to heal his son because his disciples could not do it. "And Jesus said to him, 'If you can! All things are possible for one who believes.' Immediately the father of the child cried out and said, "I believe; help my unbelief!"' (Mark 9:23-24).

Christians must believe that Jesus can do all things at all times. Moreover, to defeat the enemy of unbelief, believers must seek to have a strong prayer life and rely on God's Word when faced with what seems to be an impossible situation.

Here are several scriptures that you can use to help you defeat your unbelief. Try your best to memorize these scriptures and use them when you are faced with a situation that causes you to question God's ability to come through for you. Remember the importance of speaking the Word to your situation:

Psalm 14:1	Mark 9:23–24	James 1:5–8
Isaiah 43:10–12	John 20:29–31	
Matthew 9:28–29	Hebrews 11:6	

Faith Fighting Fear

In November 2014, my wife and I went to Israel for the second time. During the summer leading up to our trip, Israel was in a military conflict with Hamas. Deadly rockets were being fired into Israel, and the Israelite army was attacking Hamas territory. The media ran stories daily on the conflict that was taking place.

A few weeks prior to leaving for Israel, several people asked me whether I was still going on the trip. They wanted to know if I was afraid about what could happen to me. I had to explain on more than one occasion, that yes, I was still traveling to Israel, and although I was concerned about the situation in the Middle East, I knew the same God that protected us in Chicago would take care of us in Israel. Thanks to God's grace, the Lord not only protected the entire group, but he blessed us with an unforgettable spiritual experience.

At times, most Christians become afraid of something. Some believers are frightened by a bee flying around in their house, while another may be fearful of growing old and living alone. There are many fears in the world that the people of God must guard against. Loneliness, violence, diseases, and even dying are real fears that may plague believers at some point in their lives. When Christians succumb to fear, it immobilizes them from walking by faith. Fear creates a false sense that God is limited in his power and unable to deliver them through their situation.

The Bible gives examples of men and women of faith who became fearful at one time or another in their lives. Abraham feared for his life while he was traveling to Egypt. He told his wife, Sarah, that if anyone asked her who she was, she was to say that she was his sister. Abraham did not want anyone to know that Sarah was his wife because he feared Pharaoh might kill him to marry Sarah.

The prophet Elijah, after the great display of faith at Mount Carmel, feared the wicked Queen Jezebel's evil threats to kill him. She sent a messenger to tell Elijah, "So may the gods do to me and more also, if I do not make your life as the life of one of them by this time tomorrow" (1 Kings 19:2). Even the Lord's disciples in the garden of Gethsemane were struck with fear and abandoned Jesus when the chief priest and guards seized Christ (Mark 14:50).

Fear is a physical emotion that Satan uses to defeat Christians' faith, but operational faith is a spiritual virtue that is connected to the authority and power of God. How do Christians use operational faith to fight their fears?

The first step to overcoming fear is knowing that your operational faith fights fear with the Word of God, which says, "For God gave us a spirit, not of fear, but of power and love and self-control" (2 Timothy 1:7). Jesus also instructed his disciples, "And do not fear those who kill the body but cannot kill the soul. Rather fear him who can destroy both soul and body in hell" (Matthew 10:28). Every Christian must learn Bible verses and apply them to his or her own situation to conquer their fears. When you learn what scripture says regarding fear, you can then use scriptures to help you overcome your fears.

Second, when you operate your life by faith, you will be in the will of God. As a result, you do not have to be fearful of any situation. It may be God's will to allow you to be persecuted like Stephen in Acts 7 or to have you rescued from your situation, like Peter in Acts 12. The big picture is, because we are in God's will, nothing can happen to us by coincidence, luck, or fate.

Therefore, we don't have to fear. We must learn to speak the Word of God to conquer the fears in our life. When you do this, you will be using your operational faith. Remember the Pharisees and religious leaders, at various times in Jesus's ministry, attempted to kill him. Yet they could not take him before his time. Jesus knew he was doing the will of his Father and nothing could happen to him before he completed the Father's will.

Here are Bible verses that you can use to speak the Word to overcome your fears:

Psalm 27:1-3	Matthew 5:10–12	2 Timothy 1:7
Isaiah 43:1–2	Matthew 10:28–31	
Isaiah 54:17	Romans 8:31–39	

Faith Fighting a Complaining Spirit

Christians must fight daily against having a complaining spirit. Satan will try to tempt the people of God to complain about various things in their lives. The children of Israel had a major problem in this area. In Exodus 16 and 17, after God delivered them from more than four hundred years of slavery in Egypt, the Israelites complained about having no food and water.

> And the whole congregation of the people of Israel grumbled against Moses and Aaron in the wilderness, and the people of

> Israel said to them, "Would that we had died by the hand of the Lord in the land of Egypt, when we sat by the meat pots and ate bread to the full, for you have brought us out into this wilderness to kill this whole assembly with hunger" (Exodus 16:2–3).

Moses told the children of Israel, "Your grumbling is not against us but against the Lord" (Exodus 16:8).

In Exodus 17, the people did not find any water so again they complained against Moses.

> Therefore, the people quarreled with Moses and said, "Give us water to drink." And Moses said to them, "Why do you quarrel with me? Why do you test the Lord?" But the people thirsted there for water, and the people grumbled against Moses and said, "Why did you bring us up out of Egypt, to kill us and our children and our livestock with thirst?" (Exodus 17:2–3).

Complaining, grumbling, or murmuring is an enemy of operational faith because it is a weapon that Satan uses to get Christians not to trust God. When Christians complain, it exposes the deficiency in their faith. Having a complaining spirit not only shows a lack of faith in God's ability, but it also angers God. When the children of God continued to have a complaining spirit, it led to God punishing them.

This was exemplified with the children of Israel in Numbers 11:1. "And the people complained in the hearing of the Lord about their misfortunes, and when the Lord heard it, his anger was kindled, and the fire of the Lord burned among them and consumed some outlying parts of the camp." Having a complaining spirit can also lead to rebelling against God. It can cause you to lose hope and not believe that God will see you through.

As a Christian, you should always be optimistic about your situation. You may not have everything that you think you need, but be thankful for what you have. Try not to complain about things such as your job, church, or family. Remember to pray when Satan tempts you to complain and keep a positive attitude. By operating by faith, you realize that God can change your circumstances at any point in time.

A good technique to use to combat complaining is singing. Sing uplifting songs while you deal with your adversity. In Acts 16 while Paul and Silas were in a Philippian jail, the Bible says, "About midnight Paul and Silas were praying and singing hymns to God, and the prisoners were listening to them," (Acts 16:25).

If singing isn't for you, spend time reading or watching uplifting stories. This will inspire you to keep trusting God as you wait on God. Always keep the faith by demonstrating a thankful attitude. We must have an attitude that is filled with thankfulness and joy. The psalmist states in Psalm 92:1, "It is good to give thanks to the Lord, to sing praises to your name, O Most High."

You can use these scriptures to help you deal with a complaining spirit:

Exodus 17:2–6	Philippians 2:14–15	Jude 1:14-16
Numbers 11:1–2	Philippians 4:10–11	
1 Corinthians 10:9–11	Hebrews 13:5	

Faith Fighting Worry

As children of faith, we must not worry. Having a spirit of worry is closely associated with having a complaining spirit. When Christians worry, they show a lack of faith in God. As a result of worrying, there is a tendency for Christians to take matters into their own hands instead of waiting for God to resolve their situation.

In Matthew, Jesus instructed his disciples not to worry. "Therefore I tell you, do not be anxious about your life, what you will eat or what you will drink, nor about your body, what you will put on. Is not life more than food, and the body more than clothing?" (Matthew 6:25).

Jesus further stated that the Father knows exactly what his children need. He instructed them to instead focus their attention on spiritual things. Matthew 6:32–33 states, "For the Gentiles seek after all these things, and your heavenly Father knows that you need them all. But seek first the kingdom of God and his righteousness, and all these things will be added to you."

Paul the apostle also gave an example for the church, stating that he had learned to be content with whatever situation he was in (Philippians 4:11).

So many people are worried about various issues in their lives. This includes issues regarding health, family, economy, terrorist attacks, crime, and violence in their neighborhood. Even as I write this book, there are those who are worried about the possibility of a nuclear attack from North Korea. However, people of faith must not worry about these things. Instead they must utilize operational faith when faced with situations that initially causes worrying. Satan often uses worrying as a way to get God's children to have a carnal mind. He does not want the believer to face his or her situation in a spiritual or godly way. When Christians worry, it can easily progress to having a spirit of fear.

How do we as children of God fight worrying? We fight it with prayer. We fight it with reading scripture. We fight it with operational faith. This faith is rooted in knowing that God is with us no matter what we may go through. In addition, we fight worrying with the peace of God and patience. We must rely on this truth that because God loves us and understands us, he will take care of us.

Here are scriptures for you to memorize and study that will help to defeat worry:

Psalm 34:15–19
Matthew 6:25–34
Luke 12:28–31
John 14:27
John 16:32–33
Philippians 4:6–8
1 Peter 5:7

Faith Fighting Pride

Pride is a very serious enemy of our faith. Although pride can show itself in numerous ways, it can easily be hidden within the believer's life. When a child of God receives a promotion on his or her job, it can lead to pride. When a believer is wealthy and has numerous cars, houses, and other material possessions, it can create a spirit of pride. When Christians receive numerous degrees, honors, and various accolades from their peers, it can birth a spirit of pride. Additionally, when a Christian is a gifted singer or a minister is recognized for his or her exceptional preaching ability, pride can easily develop if the believer does not remember to give God the glory for what he has done. There must be a genuine humility in one's character, no matter how well he or she is blessed.

Every child of God must guard himself or herself against the sin of pride because God hates those who are lifted up in pride (Proverbs 8:13). We should remind ourselves daily of the words of Solomon. "Pride goes before destruction, and a haughty spirit before a fall" (Proverbs 16:18) "One's pride will bring him low, but he who is lowly in spirit will obtain honor" (Proverbs 29:23). When we are lifted up in pride, we allow ourselves to be used by Satan and to take on a nature like his. However, when we walk in humility, we allow ourselves to be used by Christ.

There are examples in scripture of those who could have been lifted up in pride but rather demonstrated a spirit of humility. Abraham and Moses were two men who displayed great humility as God's servants. Abraham was very wealthy but at the same time was humble in his lifestyle. Moses was a great leader but was a man who showed great humility.

If you are wealthy or feel that you have an important job and responsibilities, you must be conscious of having a humble spirit. It must be evident in your interaction with others. In other words, just because you "say" you are humble, doesn't mean that you "are" humble. Others must be the recipients of your humility.

Operational faith must fight a spirit of pride because pride lifts up the individual and does not glorify God. When Satan attacks Christians with pride, he is attempting to get believers to think that what they have achieved is the result of their own actions. The body of Christ must understand that God receives glory when we live a life of humility. We must remember that as Christians, we are instructed: "humble yourselves before the Lord, and he will exalt you" (James 4:10).

Jesus is our greatest example of someone who showed humility. He left his glory in heaven to come here to put on human clothes just to redeem man. He was born in a stable and lived a humble life. The apostle Paul said it best when he wrote,

> Have this mind among yourselves, which is yours in Christ Jesus, who, though he was in the form of God, did not count equality with God a thing to be grasped, but emptied himself, by taking the form of a servant, being born in the likeness of men. And being found in human form, he humbled himself by becoming obedient to the point of death, even death on a cross. (Philippians 2:5–8)

Read the following verses to remind you of the importance of not being prideful. Include in your daily prayer these words, "Lord, keep me humble and forgive me if my heart is filled with pride."

Proverbs 8:13	Daniel 4:34–37	1 Peter 5:6
Proverbs 16:18–19	Matthew 18:1–4	
Isaiah 66:2	James 4:6, 10	

Faith Fighting Lust

Every child of God must fight against a spirit of lust. Jesus warned his disciples about the sin of lust. He states in Matthew 5:27–28, "You have heard that it was said, 'You shall not commit adultery.' But I say to you that everyone who looks at a woman with lustful intent has already committed adultery with her in his heart."

Lust is an enemy of faith because lust wants to satisfy our worldly or sensual desires. Lust wants us to please ourselves instead of pleasing God. A person can lust for many things such as money, clothes, cars, houses, jewelry, and people. However, God wants us to ask him and patiently wait on him to give us the desires of our heart.

As Christians, we must fight lust because it is an enemy that can ruin a Christian's life, and it can even bring forth death (James 1:15). Lust is carnal, sensual, and Satan-inspired. Lust is a tool that Satan uses to make a Christian fall from a righteous state with God. Satan controls the world by lust. The apostle John wrote, "For all that is in the world—the lust of the flesh, the lust of the eyes, and the pride of life—is not of the Father but is of the world" (1 John 2:16 NKJV).

The temptation of lust can become so strong that in order not to succumb to it, Christians may have to literally run from it. The story of David and Bathsheba is one of the stories in the Bible that shows how one of God's servants succumbed to the lust of the eyes. David should have never sent for Bathsheba after seeing her bathe on the rooftop. Remember lust is of the world, while faith is of God.

In our day and time, we must be on guard against Satan using social media to create a spirit of the lust within us. Satan can generate lust within us through our cell phones, tablets, and computers. Pornography via the internet and/or television can easily transform a Christian from a moral and holy lifestyle to an immoral and lustful state of mind.

How do Christians fight against a spirit of lust? We must fight by using the Word of God, but also with godly wisdom. This means that Christians must not place themselves in situations where they are easily tempted and as a result may commit sin. They also must be ready to literally run from lust. Equally as important is that Christians must fight lust by staying away from individuals that can cause them to lust.

Proverbs 7 tells of a man who succumbed to a woman's propositions. He allowed his lust to drive him to her without considering the consequences of his actions. "With much seductive speech she persuades him; with her smooth talk she compels him" (Proverbs 7:21). As Christians, we must be determined to prevent lust from developing and having a stronghold in our lives. Therefore, we must fight fiercely to avoid situations that may cause us to lust.

Here are some scriptures that you can use to fight lust:

Matthew 5:28–30	1 Corinthians 10:13	1 John 2:15–17
Romans 1:24–27	I Timothy 6:10–11	
Romans 13:12–14	James 1:14–16	

Conclusion

When we walk by faith, it means we fight by faith. Remember Paul stated, "I have fought the good fight, I have finished the race, I have kept the faith" (2 Timothy 4:7).

We fight the enemies of faith by using the Word of God. We fight the enemy in the same way that Jesus fought Satan with Old Testament scripture (Matthew 4). Because of God's grace, we have the entire Bible, all sixty-six books, to give us fighting power to defeat the enemy.

Remember, the best defense is a great offense. We must let the Holy Spirit lead us as he led Jesus. We must be vigilant in studying scripture. We must be consistent in praying even when we don't feel like praying. We must be resilient in knowing that we have the victory. Remember Paul's words, "What then shall we say to these things? If God is for us, who can be against us?" (Romans 8:31).

Discussion Questions/Exercises

1. Name three areas of your faith that Satan often attacks you as a Christian. Next, read 1 John 2:15–17, and list the kind of behaviors that fall within the three areas. One example could be using your credit card on purchases that you don't need to buy. You would list that example under the lust of the eyes. After you have made your list, take a week to pray and ask God for strength to help you overcome these possible situations.

2. Which enemies of your faith do you need to work the hardest to defeat? Write a one- to two-page paper on how you will be victorious over them. Keep your paper for at least six months and then review it to see if you are following what you have written.

3. Explain how you can utilize the Fruit of the Spirit (Galatians 5:22–23) to help you defeat the enemies of faith?

CHAPTER 7

The Holy Spirit Empowering Operational Faith

And I will ask the Father, and he will give you another Helper, to be with you forever, even the Spirit of truth, whom the world cannot receive, because it neither sees him nor knows him. You know him, for he dwells with you and will be in you.

—John 14:16–17

Witnessing with Operational Faith

Every believer must be led by the Holy Spirit. The Holy Spirit empowers the church to move forward by faith. The Holy Spirit is in charge of God's church. He gives power to the church so we are able to do the will of God. Scripture shows that Jesus instructed his disciples to wait for the promise of the Father. "And behold, I am sending the promise of my Father upon you. But stay in the city until you are clothed with power from on high" (Luke 24:49).

Jesus knew he would no longer be physically present with his disciples and that the Holy Spirit would come to guide, teach, and comfort all of them. He also knew that in order for the disciples to be effective in witnessing for him, they would need the Holy Spirit to empower them. Acts 1:8 says, "But you will receive power when the Holy Spirit has come upon you, and you will be my witnesses in Jerusalem and in all Judea and Samaria, and to the end of the earth."

The Lord has commanded the church to be his witnesses throughout the world, which is referred to as the Great Commission. The Great Commission is a charge to the church in the first century as well as to the church in current times.

> Go therefore and make disciples of all nations, baptizing them in the name of the Father and of the Son and of the Holy Spirit, teaching them to observe all that I have commanded you. And behold, I am with you always, to the end of the age. (Matthew 28:19–20)

In order for each believer to be an effective witness, he or she must allow the Holy Spirit to direct their path by submitting their will to the authority of the Holy Spirit. When the Holy Spirit leads believers, he wants them to walk by faith and to trust God in all areas of their lives. He wants them to totally depend on him.

As we use operational faith to witness to others, the Holy Spirit will be our guide. Are you allowing the Holy Spirit to have his way in your life? If we are to be an effective witness for Christ, we must obey the Holy Spirit. As Christians follow the Holy Spirit, he will comfort and keep them as they go through life's various challenges.

After the resurrection of Christ, the apostle Peter experienced many challenges. One of them occurred when he was on a rooftop and experienced a vision. The Lord used the vision to get Peter's attention so he would be willing to go with the men who were seeking him.

While Peter was thinking about the meaning of the vision, scripture says, "The Spirit said to him, 'Behold, three men are looking for you. Rise and go down and accompany them without hesitation, for I have sent them'" (Acts 10:19–20).

Peter obeyed the Spirit by going with the men. He used operational faith by trusting God to lead him as he traveled with the men whom he did not know. When Peter got to Cornelius' house, he told everyone in the house about Jesus Christ. Peter witnessed to the Gentiles, for this was the will of God. As a result, "the Holy Spirit fell on all who heard the word" (Acts 10:44).

In our current day, the church must witness to all those who are lost in the community. We have to make a special effort, as we are led by the Holy Spirit, to reach those around us, especially our youth. There are many young people who have never attended Sunday school or Vacation Bible School nor ever heard biblical stories about Jesus. The church must realize that the same Holy Spirit who empowered the early church is the same Holy Spirit who will give saints power in current times to witness to lost souls. Let us not hesitate to obey the Spirit, as he leads us to witness in the communities that we serve.

Being Filled with the Spirit

As Christians, we must be filled with the Spirit and not be carnal-minded. When we become filled with the Spirit, it means that we allow the Spirit to control our lives. We submit to his leadership. We allow him to take over us. The Spirit filled the apostles in Acts 2, "And they were all filled with the Holy Spirit and began to speak in other tongues as the Spirit gave them utterance" (Acts 2:4). The Spirit filled the believers for the purpose of having them share the Word of God with others (Acts 2:11).

We too must share God's wonderful blessings with others. When we know God's Word, the Spirit can then lead us and speak through us. Let me caution you not to have a superficial knowledge of scripture, but to be grounded in God's Word. The Spirit will give you understanding and the ability to apply the Word of God to all situations. Jesus expected his disciples to listen and obey the Holy Spirit. When Christians submit to the control of the Holy Spirit, they will be in a position to operate by faith.

If we are to allow the Holy Spirit to control our lives, we must not grieve the Spirit by indulging in ungodly behaviors. The apostle Paul stated, "Those who are in the flesh cannot please God. You, however, are not in the flesh but in the Spirit, if in fact the Spirit of God dwells in you. Anyone who does not have the Spirit of Christ does not belong to him" (Romans 8:8–9).

When we do not regularly read the Bible and consistently pray, we limit our ability to understand what the Spirit is saying through scripture and prayer. When we become filled with the Spirit, we become more connected to God's will for our lives. Worshiping, witnessing, praying, fasting, and studying the Word of God help us to become more spiritual and reliant on God leading us. Every believer must use operational faith as the Holy Spirit controls his or her life. The Holy Spirit expects the believer to use their faith as he or she submits to him.

Walking after the Spirit

There is a song that we often sing in church that says, "Where he leads me I will follow, I'll go with him, with him, all the way." The words to this song have great meaning, if we are sincerely striving to walk after the Spirit. Jesus said, "When the Spirit of truth comes, he will guide you into all the truth" (John 16:13a).

Several years ago, the UniverSoul Circus was in town, and my wife and I took two of our grandchildren to see it. The event was held in a local park underneath a huge tent. We watched the animals and various acrobatic acts for over two hours. During most of that time, it was pouring down rain outside. However while under the tent, we did not hear the thunderstorms, get wet from the rain, or feel the intense wind.

In addition, the circus officials did not stop the show or close the park. While the weather conditions were turbulent on the outside, we enjoyed the entertainment on the inside. It wasn't until we left the circus that we learned how severe the storm had been.

I believe that trip illustrates how the Spirit provides for the church. The Spirit becomes the believers' umbrella. He covers them with his protection by sheltering them from Satan's attacks. He keeps them under his care when they are going through life's situations. He comforts them when they are faced with difficulties. This is not to suggest that Christians never have trials or hardships. However, the Spirit is present when hardships come, to help believers through them all.

Remember, we must walk after the Spirit so we will not fall prey to Satan. The Apostle Peter wrote, "Be sober-minded; be watchful. Your adversary the devil prowls around like a roaring lion, seeking someone to devour" (1 Peter 5:8).

Satan does not want Christians to walk after the Spirit or utilize operational faith. He wants believers to succumb to sin. Satan throws his darts of temptation at Christians, trying to get them to operate in the flesh. He knows that by walking in the flesh, they cannot walk in the Spirit. He tries to use the enemies of our faith to defeat our faith. Satan tries to get the believers to worry about their next meal. He tries to get them to complain about the problems that they're having at work. He tries to get them to become afraid about the crime taking place in their communities.

These are some of the reasons why Christians must walk after the Spirit. We cannot defeat Satan with our own strength. Nor can we defeat him with our Bible knowledge alone, without the Holy Spirit. We must allow the Holy Spirit to guide us as we use our faith to defeat Satan. 1 John 4:4 tells us, "Little children, you are from God and have overcome them, for he who is in you is greater than he who is in the world."

When Christians are walking after the Spirit, they are striving to please God. They know operational faith pleases God (Hebrews 11:6). It is the Christian's operational faith that reminds them that the Holy Spirit is with them regardless of the situation. The Holy Spirit reminds believers that the birds don't worry about their dinner. "Look at the birds of the air: they neither sow nor reap nor gather into barns, and yet your heavenly Father feeds them. Are you not of more value than they?" (Matthew 6:26).

The Spirit reminds believers not to complain about their circumstances, but rather to be thankful. "Give thanks in all circumstances; for this is the will of God in Christ Jesus for you" (1 Thessalonians 5:18). The Holy Spirit will remind believers not to fear the violence in the community. "I will never leave you nor forsake you" (Hebrews 13:5b).

It is important that we do not grieve or quench the Spirit. Allow him full access to your heart, daily obeying his voice as you operate by faith.

Conclusion

In the Model of Faith, the Holy Spirit is the key and power that makes the model operational. Without the believer allowing the Holy Spirit to guide him or her, there is no Model of Faith.

When we walk after the Spirit, we submit to the Spirit's authority. We rely on him daily to direct our path. As I strive to use my operational faith to follow the Spirit, I have learned that I must defeat an internal enemy, who acts like a wild stallion that never wants to be tamed. I have discovered that each day I must fight "self" from directing myself. Self is worldly, of the flesh, carnal, and naturally ungodly.

The apostle Paul said it best when he wrote, "For I do not understand my own actions. For I do not do what I want, but I do the very thing I hate" (Romans 7:15). And he further stated, "For I know that nothing good dwells in me, that is, in my flesh. For I have the desire to do what is right, but not the ability to carry it out. For I do not do the good I want, but the evil I do not want is what I keep on doing" (Romans 7:18–19).

I hope you understand like I do that there is a need to defeat self. We can defeat "self" by allowing the Spirit to have full reign over our lives. Remember, self wants to make decisions without consultation from God. Self wants to be lifted up in pride and not pray. Self wants to be free and independent of the Holy Spirit's guidance. All believers must learn how to get "self" to become a servant of the Spirit. You must get "self" under control by your devotion and commitment to serve God. Remember, the Spirit does not need our human help with spiritual matters. Our role as believers is to allow the Spirit to control us and for us to follow him. We will never be able to use our operational faith unless we crucify "self" and walk after the Spirit.

Discussion Questions/Exercises

1. Explain how you are following the guidance of the Holy Spirit.

2. Write a one-page paper explaining the relationship between the Holy Spirit and operational faith in a believer's life. Are you allowing the Holy Spirit to help you use your faith?

3. How have you grieved the Holy Spirit since you accepted Christ as your Savior? Name three things that you are currently doing or can do to help prevent this from reoccurring.

CHAPTER 8

Love Guiding Operational Faith

So now faith, hope, and love abide, these three; but the greatest of these is love.

—1 Corinthians 13:13

1 Corinthians 13 is known as the love chapter. In it, the apostle Paul expresses love as the greatest and most important spiritual virtue that a Christian can possess (verses 1–3). Love is greater than faith, prophecy, sacrifice, and speaking in tongues. "So now faith, hope, and love abide, these three; but the greatest of these is love" (1 Corinthians 13:13).

John, the beloved disciple, mentions the word *love* (or a form of it) a total of fifty-seven times in his gospel. He mentions it another fifty-two times in his general letters (English Standard Version). He felt that it was essential and expressed that God is love. And because he is love, all believers must be children of love (1 John 4:8).

Love plays a preeminent role in the model of faith, and without authentic love being demonstrated in the believer's life, he or she cannot live by faith. Love commands action just as operational faith does. James wrote, "Faith by itself, if it does not have works, is dead" (James 2:17).

John likewise stated, "Little children, let us not love in word or talk but in deed and in truth" (1 John 3:18). In looking at the impact of love on operational faith, it is important to note that you first must have a love relationship with the Father, Son, and Holy Spirit. Jesus summed it up by saying, "And you shall love the Lord your God with all your heart and with all your soul and with all your mind and with all your strength" (Mark 12:30).

Love Is the Greatest Spiritual Virtue

The greatest love that has ever been shown is the Father loving us enough to sacrifice his only Son to die for us. The Father gave us Jesus so we could have eternal life. St. John 3:16, which is one of the greatest verses in the Bible says, "For God so loved the world, that he gave his only Son, that whoever believes in him should not perish but have eternal life." Love is the greatest spiritual virtue that a Christian can have because love is the essence of who God is.

Operational faith is driven by God's love and demonstrated by the believer's love that he or she has for God. Because we love God, we keep his commandments and live by faith. If we love God, it is imperative that we show our love for the church (every true believer). John wrote, "Beloved, if God so loved us, we also ought to love one another" (1 John 4:11). Our love for others must be shown in a way that is authentic and sincere. In like manner, operational faith must be shown by our actions.

Jesus was driven by love. His love for the Father and his love for us is what drove him to die for us. At the onset of Jesus's ministry, the Father expressed his love for him by saying, "This is my beloved Son, with whom I am well pleased" (Matthew 3:17). The Father loved the Son; the Son loved the Father. Jesus and the Father had a perfect relationship of love. The church too must have a relationship of love.

Every believer must have the love of God flowing from him or her as he or she lives his or her life. Is God's love exemplified through you? If you don't have the love of Jesus flowing from your life daily, there is a deficiency in your faith. What you claim to do in the name of Jesus is futile, as expressed by Solomon in Ecclesiastes 1:14, "I have seen everything that is done under the sun, and behold, all is vanity and a striving after wind."

Love Commissions Faith

Operational faith works because of the power of love. The love of God commissions faith. It fuels and drives our faith. Love is the main spiritual virtue that must be attached to the believer's faith. Paul states, "For in Christ Jesus neither circumcision nor uncircumcision counts for anything, but only faith working through love" (Galatians 5:6).

In chapter 2, we discussed the principle within the model of faith that deals with comprehending God's Voice/God Speaks. We also discussed the three components that make up that principle (the voice of God, the Bible, and obedience). In essence, love is embedded in the principle. The love of God and the love of Christ is what operates our faith.

Jesus said to his disciples, "If you love me keep my commandments" (John 14:15). To love Jesus means to obey him, doing those things that please him. When we do those things that please him, we demonstrate our love for him. That is what makes faith operational.

John 14:21 says, "Whoever has my commandments and keeps them, he it is who loves me. And he who loves me will be loved by my Father, and I will love him and manifest myself to him." Because there is a love relationship between the Father and the Son, there also must be a love relationship between God and his children. The people of God must express their love for God in worship and in fellowship with one another.

When the church lives by faith, she lives by obeying the words of Christ, putting into action all that the Lord has instructed her to do. What kind of relationship do you have with other Christians? Do you want to be in fellowship with your brothers and sisters in Christ? Do you feel that there is a need to work with other Christians in ministry?

John wrote in 1 John 3:17, "But if anyone has the world's goods and sees his brother in need, yet closes his heart against him, how does God's love abide in him?" God wants his church to show love toward saints and sinners. He does not receive glory from our lip service, but from our love-driven good actions toward others. Operational faith is what we use to demonstrate our love for God. When we feed the hungry, clothe the naked, visit the sick, and visit those in prison, we are living out our faith.

However, our acts of faith must be executed from a heart of love. Our love for God directs our faith because we have a desire to please him. As we walk by faith, we walk in love. Paul highlighted this point when he said to the Ephesians, "And walk in love, as Christ loved us and gave himself up for us, a fragrant offering and sacrifice to God" (Ephesians 5:2). Paul also tells the church to allow Christ to dwell in their hearts by faith and instructs them to be rooted and grounded in love (Ephesians 3:17).

A Love Relationship

Every believer must work on improving his or her love relationship with Christ. You may feel that you're doing a great job with loving God, and you might be. However, there is always room for improvement. Spending quality time in prayer and studying God's Word are essential in building the type of love relationship with the Lord that we should have. Consistent praying should bring us closer to God, as we share with him all our heart's desires.

As we study God's Word, we learn about others who loved God by the way in which they lived their lives. Jesus took time with his disciples to teach them the importance of loving one another as well as loving their enemies. Following his resurrection, Jesus took time with Peter. Jesus wanted Peter to express his love for him by reaching others in ministry.

Jesus asked Peter three times if he loved him. Each time, Peter responded that he did love him. From this interaction, we learn that Jesus wanted Peter to show his love by engaging himself in ministry with people that God would place in his life (John 21).

The love relationship that we have with God must be authenticated by how we treat our church family. God takes notice of how our love for his church is shown. John, the beloved disciple, wrote, "If anyone says, 'I love God,' and hates his brother, he is a liar; for he who does not love his brother whom he has seen cannot love God whom he has not seen" (1 John 4:20).

One of the most exceptional ways that I have witnessed God's love was through my mother while I was a child going up. My father served in the military and was often away from home for long periods of time. Although we had extended family members around us, my mother's love stood out each and every day as she did her best to raise my sisters and me. She regularly worked a job for eight hours, came home to make sure we had a delicious home-cooked meal, and even took time to do special things to show her love. I still remember waiting for my mother to come home from work because she would often bring us special treats.

Although seemingly simple to some, it made us feel loved. My mother taught us about God and made it mandatory for us to attend Sunday school. She provided everything that she could to ensure that we had the necessities for school and church. Although we were far from being considered wealthy, she made sure we had nice things to wear and a beautiful home. She shared her love with us every day, not just by saying the words "I love you," but also by the things that she did for us. I am forever indebted to my mother for all the love she showed us.

A Love-Driven Church

For several years, I have talked to my congregation about being a love-driven church. A love-driven church shows their love for God by the way they treat one another as well as how they show love to the community.

A love-driven church is not simply a nice "motto" to be placed at the end of a church name, but it is about showing and sharing the love of God with its membership and community.

Every Christian church should strive to be a love-driven church because Jesus said, "By this all people will know that you are my disciples, if you have love for one another" (John 13:35). A love-driven congregation understands that God's love must be proven by their actions. It's about doing the will of God by demonstrating the power of love to others. It reaches beyond the church's walls to help address the various needs of the community.

Some of the ways that our church has tried to show love to our community is by sponsoring an annual Thanksgiving community dinner, Friday night movies for youth, community job readiness training and placement, clothing giveaways, and free school supplies.

Scripture gives numerous examples of love-driven individuals who showed their love in different ways. In the book of Genesis, Jacob loved Rachel. His love was displayed when he agreed to work seven years for Rachel, and the seven years seemed just like a few days to him. When Jacob found out that Laban had tricked him and instead gave him his oldest daughter, Leah, to marry, he was still driven by his love for Rachel and worked another seven years for her.

Moses taught the children of Israel to be a love-driven congregation and instructed them numerous times in the book of Deuteronomy to love God. "You shall love the Lord your God with all your heart and with all your soul and with all your might" (Deuteronomy 6:5). He also stated,

> And now, Israel, what does the Lord your God require of you, but to fear the Lord your God, to walk in all his ways, to love him, to serve the Lord your God with all your heart and with all your soul, and to keep the commandments and statutes of the Lord, which I am commanding you today for your good? (Deuteronomy 10:12–13)

Israel was expected to love God with everything they had and then go about doing his will because of their love for him. Another story of a love-driven person was Ruth. Her love for Naomi, her mother-in-law, was great. Ruth was willing to leave her own country and people and follow Naomi back to her country, a land with which Ruth was not familiar (Ruth 1).

Because Ruth was driven by love, God blessed her with a son, who was the grandfather of King David. The greatest love-driven person of all was Jesus our Savior. His entire ministry was love driven. He was driven by love when he healed the sick, raised the dead, and had compassion on the multitudes and fed them. He was driven by love when he allowed himself (though not guilty of any crime) to be persecuted and killed on the cross in our place, all because he loved us. Christ has given the church an example to follow in his love.

Conclusion

What are you doing in your life to show that you are love driven? Who are you helping? How is your church showing love for its members? Is the church remembering the words of Christ when he said, "This is my commandment, that you love one another as I have loved you" (John 15:12).

We must love the members of our congregation that may not speak to us on Sunday when they see us. Remember, the Bible is a love story from Genesis to Revelation. I personally have come to discover that the letter "L" in the word *love* is symbolic. The vertical line in the letter "L" represents our relationship of love to God, loving him with all that we have (heart, mind, body, and soul). The horizontal line in the letter "L" represents the relationship of love that we should show toward each other. When we live our lives by love, we operate our lives by faith because God's love is what powers faith.

Discussion Questions/Exercises

1. What has helped you the most in growing your love for God? Write three ways that you express your love for God.
2. Do you love to be around God's people? Do you love to serve others? Develop your love relationship with God. Write down seven ways you will demonstrate love for God's church.
3. Give three examples of love-driven people in scripture that were not mentioned in the chapter. Explain how their example can be shown in your life today.

Chapter 9

Understanding God's Will: Part 2

And this is the confidence that we have toward him, that if we ask anything according to his will he hears us. And if we know that he hears us in whatever we ask, we know that we have the requests that we have asked of him.

—1 John 5:14–15

In chapter 1, we discussed understanding God's will and what it means to complete his will. In this final chapter, I would like to suggest another area of God's will that plays an important part in understanding the will of God. When Christians use operational faith, they are pleasing God because they are doing those things that he has told them to do.

In essence, they are in the will of God. They are being led by the Holy Spirit as they accomplish the assignment that God intended for them. When we please God by living a life of faith, we must then understand that God says to us, "What do you want me to do for you?" In other words, God says, "Tell me how I can bless you because you are pleasing me by doing my will." I have always considered this as God honoring man's will.

One of the best examples of God honoring man's will is found in 1 Kings 3. Solomon was a young king over Israel who succeeded his father,

David. In 1 Kings 3, God asks Solomon how he could bless him. "At Gibeon the Lord appeared to Solomon in a dream by night, and God said, 'Ask what I shall give you'" (1 Kings 3:5). God's will was to bless Solomon. All he needed to do was to tell God what he wanted. God wanted Solomon to have the desires of his heart. It is important to note that Solomon pleased the Lord to get this kind of response from God.

Prior to God saying to Solomon "Ask what I shall give you," the writer of Kings says, "Solomon loved the Lord, walking in the statutes of David his father, only he sacrificed and made offerings at the high places" (1 Kings 3:3). Solomon's love for God and his ability to obey God, although he was not perfect, caused him to receive the favor of the Lord. As we operate our lives by faith, we live according to the Bible, and this pleases God.

As we please God, we place ourselves in a position where we can ask God for various things. A Christian's faithful living gets God's attention, and God asks, "What do you want me to do for you?" Many Christians may not understand God's will in this way, but many biblical passages support this understanding.

Two biblical examples that support this are found in the book of Psalms. In Psalm 1:1–3, the blessed man who delights himself in the law of the Lord pleases God, and God says to him, "In all that he does, he prospers" (Psalm 1:3b). God wants every Christian to do his will. He wants all to live a life of obedience to his Word and to know that he will bless everyone for his or her faithfulness.

In Psalm 37, David writes, "Trust in the Lord, and do good; dwell in the land and befriend faithfulness" (Psalm 37:3). In the next verse, he states, "Delight yourself in the Lord, and he will give you the desires of your heart" (Psalm 37:4). David understood that the person who pleases God can ask God for what he or she wants, and God will do it. In addition to the above scriptures cited, there are also supportive passages found in the New Testament.

Mary's Miracle

In John 2, we learn of the first miracle depicted that Jesus performed. It gives an account of a wedding feast in Cana, which was attended by Jesus, his mother, Mary, and his disciples. During the celebration, the wine ran out. When Jesus's mother learned of the embarrassing situation, she informed Jesus. However, Jesus did not want to become involved and told his mother, "Woman, what does this have to do with me? My hour has not yet come" (John 2:4).

Jesus seemed to be saying to his mother the time for him to do miracles had not come. I have always looked at this first miracle of Jesus as Mary's miracle. It was her operational faith that commanded change to occur. Mary said to the servants, "Do whatever he tells you" (John 2:5). Although we do not have a written account of Jesus's life between the age of twelve and thirty, Mary has been there.

For Mary to say these words suggests that she knew Jesus could do something that would help solve the problem. It is possible that Mary knew that Jesus's voice commands power. Her words, "do whatever he tells you," is a statement of affirmation. She believed that her son Jesus could change the situation. Jesus tells the servants to fill the water pots with water. His spoken words were the voice of God, and as result, water was turned into wine.

We may look at this miracle simply as Jesus honoring the request of his mother so the groom and bride would not be embarrassed about running out of wine. However, it has a deeper meaning. Operational faith took place. Jesus gave Mary the desires of her heart.

I would like to suggest that Jesus was saying to his mother, "I will do this miracle because of your faith," or to say it another way, "Mother, I will do your will because you have done my will." Jesus was a perfect son and, as such, submitted himself to his earthy parents. Although scripture does not specifically tell us how Mary was as a mother, we know God himself chose her to be Jesus's mother.

Let me explain this spiritual principle another way. When our children were growing up, my wife and I gave each of them chores to do around the house. Our daughters' chores were to clean the kitchen and their room and wash the dishes. Our son's chores were to clean the bathroom and his room and empty the garbage. When they completed their chores, they often asked if they could watch television or play outside. We would always ask them if they finished their chores and homework. If they had completed them, we allowed them to watch television or go outside and play with their friends. In addition, we did not mind buying them toys and other things that they wanted because they obeyed what we asked them to do. We were pleased with their behavior (obedience to following our instructions), and as a result, it gave them an opportunity to receive some of the things that they wanted.

A Christian's Will inside of God's Will

Within the will of God is that his children's will be done. The apostle John wrote, "And whatever we ask we receive from him, because we keep his commandments and do what pleases him" (1 John 3:22). There are Christians who have overlooked or have not understood this verse. God's will is not just for us to keep his commandments. It is also hearing him say to his children, "Because you have obeyed me and loved me, you can ask what you want, and I'll do it for you."

It is important that we understand that when we ask God for things, we're asking it based on our love relationship with him. Because we love him, we are not trying to be disobedient to what he has told us to do in scripture, but rather we always have in our mind to please God. We are not trying to ask God for permission to rob a bank, win the lottery, cheat on our spouse, or evade paying taxes or anything that is sinful because these things would be going against what the Bible teaches.

Another scripture similar to 1 John 3:22 is found in 1 John 5:14–15. "And this is the confidence that we have toward him, that if we ask anything according to his will he hears us. And if we know that he hears us in whatever we ask, we know that we have the requests that we have asked of him."

Again, this passage supports Christians asking God for something according to his will. Within the will of God, we can ask God for things that are in his will or things that please him. Further, James mentions the prayer of faith can save the sick and the prayer of a righteous person has great power (James 5:15–16). God blesses the righteous person who prays in faith, and he answers his or her prayer. When we use operational faith, we can petition God, and he will be open to answering us according to his will.

God wants us to ask him for things. If he did not, neither John nor Jesus would have stated it. Jesus states, "Ask, and it will be given to you; seek, and you will find; knock, and it will be opened to you. For everyone who asks receives, and the one who seeks finds, and to the one who knocks it will be opened" (Matthew 7:7–8).

Have you asked the Lord for something recently? Have you learned to pray according to his will? *Do you understand that inside of God's will is his permission to have our will be done?* In this same passage, Jesus also tells his disciples, "If you then, who are evil, know how to give good gifts to your children, how much more will your Father who is in heaven give good things to those who ask him!" (Matthew 7:11). The Father is waiting to give us good gifts!

Important to note that there are other passages that illustrate this same spiritual principle. In the book of Genesis, when Adam and Eve were pleasing the Lord prior to the fall of man, God gave Adam the right to name all of the animals that he had created. The text says, "And every bird of the heavens and brought them to the man to see what he would call them. And whatever the man called every living creature, that was its name." Adam used his will to operate within God's will.

Adam freely made decisions to do what he wanted to do. Although this occurred prior to the fall of man, we can still learn from it. God blesses his servants when they have a love relationship with him and are obedient to him. The Bible gives additional examples where God allowed the believer's will to be done. Two examples are found in 2 Kings 6 and Matthew 9.

In 2 Kings 6, the prophet Elisha prayed that his servant might see that those who were with them were greater than those that were with the Syrian army. God granted Elisha's request. In this same passage, Elisha prayed that the Lord would strike the Syrian army with blindness, and God caused them to lose their vision. In both instances, God knew what Elisha was going to do before he did it. So in one respect, Elisha was doing what God wanted him to do. However, because God gives man free will, man has the ability to make choices and decide for himself. Elisha's will was in keeping with God's will.

In Matthew 9, a woman had a blood disorder for twelve years. She believed that all she needed to do was touch a small part of Jesus's clothes and she would no longer have her disorder. Her will was to be healed. She used operational faith by pushing her way through the crowd. Although she faced difficulty getting to Jesus, she pushed on until she accomplished her goal. After she touched Jesus's garment, he commented, "Take heart, daughter; your faith has made you well." And instantly the woman was made well" (Matthew 9:22).

You may be wondering how you too can get God to honor your will. My question to you is, "Are you doing God's will?" The dean of preachers, Charles Hadden Spurgeon, is quoted as saying, "When your will is God's will, you will have your will."[10] I agree with this statement because it is not until you learn to love God and want to please him by obeying his Word that you then discover God saying to you, "What do you want me to do for you?" God's will is that we keep his commandments. By living by his commandments (Bible), he then allows our will to be done.

How do you get your bills paid off, purchase a new car, buy a new home, marry the right person, and even lose weight and stay in shape? First of all, remember that God gives us the desires of our heart as well as takes care of our needs. You must believe that God wants the very best for your life, even though you may not have the very best at this present moment.

---

[10] Charles Hadden Spurgeon

It is so important to work on your love relationship with Christ. As previously stated in chapter 8, our love relationship is developed when we communicate daily with the Lord through prayer and Bible study. As we find ourselves in the will of God, pleasing him by the way we live, he will place on our hearts to ask him for what we want him to do for us. When this happens, do not be shy to petition God for the desires of your heart.

During your prayer time, tell the Lord your request. This is what I did when I wanted to take a trip to Israel. He not only blessed me with one trip to Israel but allowed me to go twice. I asked God to allow me to go back to school to receive my doctoral degree. I waited patiently for him to open the door, and he did. We must remember that Jesus loves us and wants the very best for us. Because we're faithful children committed to him, he will not only give us our needs but also many of our wants.

Try to understand this spiritual principle another way. When God gives us our will, it is just an extension of his will. When we live for God and obey his Word, he gives us permission to determine how we want him to bless us. Jesus told his disciples, "Whatever you ask in my name, this I will do, that the Father may be glorified in the Son. If you ask me anything in my name, I will do it" (John14:13–14).

It is important to ask what we want in the name of Jesus. Yet we need to also note that God wants us to do our part in bringing it to pass. If I desire to have a new car, he wants me to save money or to make sure that the monthly payment fits into my budget. God does not want his children to be stressed out or worried about their bills, health, or other situations in life.

If we ask God to allow us to lose weight and become healthy, we must do our part. We must become better disciplined by eating the right types of food and exercising. God will give us some of the things that we want, but we must be faithful in doing our part in making it to come to pass. This is where operational faith comes in. Remember the ten lepers. They cried out to the Lord to have mercy on them? Jesus told them, "Go and show yourselves to the priests" (Luke 17:14). Their part was to obey the

Lord by "going." In the process of them "going" or following Jesus's instructions, they became healed.

In another passage, two blind men followed Jesus into a house and cried out loudly to him for mercy. They did their part by following Jesus into the house. They were healed because of their belief in Jesus. Remember, God is in the business of giving good gifts to his children. This is his will. The apostle James states, "Every good gift and every perfect gift is from above, coming down from the Father of lights, with whom there is no variation or shadow due to change" (James 1:17).

Conclusion

God's will is a wonderful place to be for the child of God. The singer Karen Clark Sheard recorded a song, "The Will of God." Some of the lyrics are, "The safest place in the whole wide world, is in the will of God. Though trials be great, and the way seems hard, it's in the will of God. It may be on a mountain peak, or in the valley low, but wherever it may be. If God says 'go,' go."

The words to this song capture the true understanding of a Christian who is living in God's will. Every believer must understand that the best place to be is in the will of God.

Discovering God's will for your life should be your lifelong mission. As you learn how to discern God's voice, the next step is to obey it. "But be doers of the word, and not hearers only, deceiving yourselves" (James 1:22). God has commanded us to not just hear his word, but more importantly to do what it says. When God has given you a green light to go, you precede by operational faith.

Operational faith takes you forward so you can accomplish God's will. As you operate by faith, at times you will encounter roadblocks, storms, and various temptations. Your faith will face enemies of faith, but don't give up the fight. Fight with operational faith. Also remember that your faith relies on the two friends of faith, prayer and patience, to support your faith. Prayer says to tell God about your situation while patience says to wait on God to direct you through your situation.

When the Holy Spirit directs you forward, you move by operational faith, always recalling what God has said to you. Keep in mind how God's love inspires your faith to operate according to his will. Your goal is to accomplish God's will for your life, to complete it. Remember when God was creating the world? He did not stop after day one or day two, but he created everything in six days and rested the seventh day. The Father completed everything he intended to do.

When Jesus came into the world, his mission was not just to preach and teach, heal the sick, and raise the dead, but it was also to die for the sins of the world and be resurrected from the dead on Sunday morning. Jesus completed the Father's will, and so must we! As you live your life by God's Word, you will discover that it pleases God when you ask him what he can do for you. You will also discover when you live by operational faith, your faith in God leads to blessings.

Remember these words from the apostle Paul. "I have been crucified with Christ. It is no longer I who live, but Christ who lives in me. And the life I now live in the flesh I live by faith in the Son of God, who loved me and gave himself for me" (Galatians 2:20).

For more than twenty years, this book, in some shape or form, has been on my heart to write. Also during this time, the Lord placed the "Faith Saying" in my spirit. As you discover God's will for your life, continue to operate your life by faith. Remember the words of the faith saying to motivate you to complete God's will for your life.

Have I yet found myself in God's will?

Have I yet lost myself in his trust?

Is my faith solid in going forward where I cannot see?

Discussion Questions/Exercises

1. How do you know if your life is in the will of God? Did you complete the review questions in chapter 1? What gives you the confidence that you are pleasing God?

2. What have you asked God to do that he has not yet done? What must you do to bring it to fruition? How will you use your operational faith to achieve your goal(s)?

3. Write down three scriptures that illustrate how God allowed a believer's will to become his will. Did prayer and/or patience play a role in receiving God's blessings?

Appendix

Sermons

The following sermons are messages that I have preached to congregations that in some way highlight operational faith. It should be noted that all sermon scripture quotations are from the The Holy Bible, English Standard Version (ESV) or King James Version (KJV).

If you are a minister, you may use these sermons with your own modifications as the Holy Spirit leads you.

Sermon 1: "When Rocks Cry Out" (Luke 19:37–40)

Introduction

According to science, "The Earth's outer solid layer, the lithosphere, the crust, is made of rock. Rocks have been used by mankind throughout history. Since the Stone Age, rocks have been used for tools. The minerals and metals found in rocks have been essential to human civilization."

Science also tells us that when the Earth first formed, 4.6 billion years ago, it was a hot ball of molten rock and metal. All over the world, the earth is made up of various types of rocks. This makes me think of Psalm 24:1. "The earth is the Lord's and the fullness thereof, the world and those who dwell therein."

When my wife and I were in Jerusalem, we saw very large stones (or rocks) that had been excavated from centuries ago. They were stones that had fallen from the temple. Some of you may recall Jesus's words in Matthew 24:1–2.

> Jesus left the temple and was going away, when his disciples came to point out to him the buildings of the temple. But he answered them, "You see all these, do you not? Truly, I say to you, there will not be left here one stone upon another that will not be thrown down."

Jesus said these words during the last week of his earthly ministry. The week started out with celebration. Jews from all around the land had come to celebrate the Passover.

The first day of the week, Sunday, was a day of joy and jubilation. It was a time for the Jews to remember what God had done for their ancestors. We too should remember what God has done for us. We need to remember that God has not brought us part of the way in our lives, but all the way.

Point 1: A Day of Praise

Jesus's triumphal entry into Jerusalem was the first Palm Sunday. It was a day of praise. The text says, "The whole multitude of his disciples began to rejoice and praise God" (Luke 19:37).

Every day that we wake up in the morning should be a day to praise God.

The people had a reason to praise God. Scripture says, "For all the mighty works that they had seen" (Luke 19:37b). Do you have a reason to praise God?

We often complain so much that we fail to realize how blessed we are. It could be worse than what it currently is. If God does not do anything else for you, he has already done enough.

The people with a loud voice said, "Blessed is the King who comes in the name of the Lord! Peace in heaven and glory in the highest" (Luke 19:38). Jesus was indeed a king. Do you remember in John 6 the people wanted to make Jesus a king after he fed them?

However, Jesus did not come to be an earthly king. Every child of God should know that Jesus is the King of Kings. Revelations 19:16 tells us, "On his robe and on his thigh, he has a name written, King of kings and Lord of lords." If you know him as your king, he must also be lord of your life. That means you must submit to his authority. Jesus must be first in your life.

And if we really have Jesus in our lives, he will be there for us when we are going through troubled times. A popular gospel song is "Long as I Got King Jesus." In it, the songwriter penned these words, "I been lied on, cheated, talked about, mistreated. I been buked, scorned. Talked about, sure as you're born. I been up, down. Almost to the ground. Long as I got King Jesus. Long as I got him, I don't need nobody else."

I believe that the songwriter understood that although man would let him down, Jesus would never let him down. The first Palm Sunday was a day exaltation, a day of great praise.

Point 2: The Pharisees' Opposition against Jesus

It's amazing how, when you are having a good time, there are always some disenchanted folks in the crowd. There are always some "haters" around. For example, you may save your money to buy a new car. You pray about it, and God finally blesses you to buy it. Yet there will be some people who can't find it within themselves to say something nice. They don't want you to prosper seemingly better than them and would rather look at you funny than say congratulations.

Some of the Pharisees in the crowd did not want Jesus to be in the limelight either. They were nothing more than Satan's servants. They had the audacity to say to Jesus, "Teacher, rebuke your disciples" (Luke 19:39).

The Pharisees did not want the people to glorify Jesus. They were jealous and envious that the people were reverencing Jesus. He had become the center of attention and not them. We must be careful that our lack of praising God isn't a step toward supporting Satan.

Satan wants us to be quiet in the church. He doesn't want us to shout for God, but we should know that the enemy's been defeated with a shout. In Joshua 6:20, Joshua tells the Israelites to shout to win the city of Jericho, "As soon as the people heard the sound of the trumpet, the people shouted a great shout, and the wall fell down flat." God gave Israel the victory!

Also in Job 8:21–22, it says, "He will yet fill your mouth with laughter, and your lips with shouting. Those who hate you will be clothed with shame, and the tent of the wicked will be no more." The psalmist writes in Psalm 47:1, "Clap your hands, all peoples! Shout to God with loud songs of joy!"

Saints, you should shout for the Lord! Shout out to him for all that he has done for you. Your deliverance my come through your shout! Your victory may come through your shout! Your healing may come through your shout!

Part 3: Jesus's Words of Confirmation

Jesus answered the Pharisees, "I tell you, if these were silent, the very stones would cry out" (Luke 19:40). The King James Version says it this way, "I tell you that, if these should hold their peace, the stones would immediately cry out."

Have you thought about stones crying out? It was good for the people to praise Jesus. It was the righteous will of God that adoration and glory be given to the Son of God. In addition, the prophet Habakkuk spoke similar words of stones crying out when he stated, "For the stone will cry out from the wall, and the beam from the woodwork respond" (Habakkuk 2:11).

We look at rocks as being substances or types of material, but God sees all of his creation as entities in which he can communicate with. That's because all his creation is under his divine control. Nothing is impossible with God. All things exist because of his spoken Word.

Therefore, the wind and the water are under his authority, and they know his voice. Jesus on the Sea of Galilee spoke to the wind. Mark records in his gospel, "And he arose, and rebuked the wind, and said unto the sea, Peace, be still. And the wind ceased, and there was a great calm" (Mark 4:39). Because God has all power and authority, his creation obeys him. In Nahum 1:3b, the prophet Nahum states, "The LORD hath his way in the whirlwind and in the storm, and the clouds *are* the dust of his feet." God can do the impossible!

Why did Jesus say the rocks would cry out and not the turtles or the frogs? While they too could have cried out, I believe that rocks being an inanimate object speaks more to the omnipotence of God. It further indicates that if one creation doesn't give God glory, another one will … even rocks. When rocks cry out, it means that man would have failed his responsibility to glorify the God of this universe. It means man has failed his responsibility to praise his Creator and his Redeemer.

Jeremiah and Isaiah both recorded that God is the potter and we his people are the clay. And God can do with us whatsoever he chooses.

Conclusion

Jesus rode victoriously into Jerusalem, but days later, the tide had turned, and the people were chanting "Crucify him! Crucify him!"

The Romans persecuted our Savior, but what they didn't realize was that they were trying to destroy a rock. Paul the apostle wrote in 1 Corinthians 10:4, "And did all drink the same spiritual drink: for they drank of that spiritual Rock that followed them: and that Rock was Christ."

Most rocks are hard and tough and can withstand a storm. They can last forever. In Matthew 7, Jesus shared with his disciples about a man who built his house on a rock, and his house survived the storm because its foundation was built on a rock. Jesus is our rock! Jesus said to his disciples, “On this rock I will build my church” (Matthew 16:18).

Hannah in her prayer said, “There is none holy like the Lord: for there is none besides you; there is no rock like our God” (1 Samuel 2:2). And the psalmist wrote, “Oh come, let us sing unto the Lord: Let us make a joyful noise to the rock of our salvation” (Psalm 95:1).

Jesus is the rock. He is the rock of our salvation! He was the true rock who spoke to Moses to speak to the rock, and water came forth. The words to the song “The Solid Rock” says it perfectly:

> My hope is built on nothing less
>
> Than Jesus' blood and righteousness;
>
> I dare not trust the sweetest frame,
>
> But wholly lean on Jesus' name.
>
> *On Christ, the solid Rock, I stand;*
>
> All other ground is sinking sand,
>
> All other ground is sinking sand …

Is he your rock today? One Friday morning, they marched our rock up an old rugged hill called Calvary. They nailed our rock on a cross and held it up high. Some dared our rock to come down from the cross, but he stayed there until he died. Then they put our rock into a borrowed rock and sealed the rock with a rock. But on Sunday morning, our great rock got up, moved the rock, and declared that he has all power!

Oh, what a great God we serve!

Sermon 2: "A Powerful Word" (Luke 4:31–36; Luke 9:1–2)

Our Lord and Savior Jesus Christ came into the world to do his Father's will. His mission was to save men and women from their sins.

Dr. Luke records in Luke 19:10, "For the Son of Man is come to seek and to save those which were lost." Our Savior was a Man of God and a man of action. He was a man of mighty and powerful words. His words could change people lives. His words caused men and women to repent of their sins and allowed them to come to a forgiving and loving heavenly Father.

During the course of Jesus's ministry, Matthew tells us of an occasion where our Savior saw a multitude. He went up into a mountain, and his disciples came to him. While on the mountain, he gave them a sermon, which is known as the "Sermon on the Mount." In this sermon, Jesus spoke to them some very powerful words (Matthew 5–6).

> Blessed are the poor in spirit: for theirs is the kingdom of heaven … Blessed are the pure in heart: for they shall see God … Let your light so shine before men, that they may see your good works, and glorify your father in heaven … Love your enemies, bless them that curse you, do good to them that hate you, and pray for them which despitefully use you.

He told them when you pray to say, "Our Father which art in heaven, Hallowed be thy name."

Likewise, we should not forget that our Lord said, "But seek ye first the kingdom of God and his righteousness."

When he had ended these sayings, the people were astonished at his doctrine. For he taught them as one having authority and not as scribes. Yes, it's true that Jesus had powerful words. But what about us? What about you and me? Where is the power in our words?

How many times have you heard someone say, "I don't know how I'm going to make it? I just have too many bills to pay"? We complain about the weather. At times we hear those who say, "It's too cold. It's too hot. Why did it rain today?" We are worried about our children, our jobs, our health, and other things. But the Lord would have us to know that if we are children of God, then we should be children of hope and faith.

Do you know that you can defeat yourself by the words you say? If you're always talking negatively and only see life in a pessimistic and close-minded way, then that type of spirit will drive your life. You will always be talking about what you cannot do if you don't speak positive words.

I remember watching a football game in the company of family members. There was five minutes remaining in the game, and my team was losing.

One of my relatives said, "Oh well, the game is over. Your team's going to lose."

When I heard that statement, I started to get upset and said, "Wait a minute! There's still five minutes left in the game. Don't give up on my team. Anything can happen. My team may be losing, but I believe that anything can happen to change the score. I believe all things are possible."

Where is the "hope" in our words? Where is our belief that God can work out our situation? Some of us are giving up on God. If anyone should speak positive words, words of encouragement, words of determination, it should be the children of God.

Remember the Hebrew boys and the words they proclaimed in Daniel 3:17? "Our God whom we serve is able to deliver us from the burning fiery furnace." Their words were words of faith and hope.

As we look at the text, in Luke 4:31, it reads, "Jesus went to Capernaum, a city in Galilee, and on the Sabbath day, he taught the people. And they were astonished at his doctrine: for his word was with power." Jesus's words were with authority, and he taught the people with power.

He also spent a significant time teaching his disciples. He taught them because he wanted his disciples to become like him. He wanted them to be men who could "speak the Word, teach the Word, and preach the Word."

That's why he took time to teach them. And the Bible tells us that he gave them practice time, time to experience highs and lows of ministry. In other words, he gave them an opportunity to preach a powerful word.

Scripture tells us in Luke 9:1–2, "Then he called his 12 disciples together, and gave them power and authority over all devils, and to cure diseases. And he sent them to preach the kingdom of God, and to heal the sick."

How does the church develop a powerful Word today? How do we obtain spiritual power? We must have a closeness to God that is developed through prayer and fasting. I have discovered that many Christians don't spend enough time in prayer.

Do you realize that we are in a spiritual battle, facing a real spiritual enemy? Peter did not want to deny Christ three times. He told Jesus that he was ready to go with him to prison and even to die for him, but Peter didn't have enough spiritual power. Jesus told him that Satan's desire was to have him, to sift him as wheat. Yet Jesus further told him, "I have prayed for you that your faith should not fail" (Luke 22:32).

A devoted prayer life is a prerequisite for a person with a powerful word. Having a devoted prayer life sets the stage for the Word of God to be a part of you, so you can "speak" a powerful word.

There are many instances where Dr. Luke records that Jesus prayed. In Luke 5:16, Jesus withdraws himself into the wilderness to pray. Luke 6:12 states that Jesus went out into a mountain to pray and continued all night in prayer to God. In Luke 9:18, Luke states Jesus was alone praying. Also in Luke 9:28, we discover that the entire experience of the transfiguration came out of the prayer meeting that Jesus and his inner circle were holding.

What am I saying? Jesus spent quality time praying to the Father. Now what does that tell us?

The problem we are having today is that there are too many weak Christians in our churches, and where there are weak Christians, there will be envy, strife, jealousy, and confusion. Too many Christians can't get a prayer through because when they get through praying, they have already given up on what they prayed for by expressing doubt.

If you're lacking a dedicated and consistent prayer life, then you're lacking spiritual power. You can't have power in your words when you don't have power in your prayer life.

One of the great preachers of the nineteenth century was Charles Haddon Spurgeon. He stated, "We cannot all argue, but we can all pray; we cannot all be leaders, but we can all be pleaders; we cannot all be mighty in rhetoric, but we can all be prevalent in prayer."[11]

Jesus wanted his disciples to follow his example. He wanted them to be men of prayer as well as men of faith. Remember the story about the man who had the demonic son? The boy had seizures and was falling into the fire and water. That's how uncontrollable it was. His father brought him to the disciples for them to heal him, but they were unable to do it. They were powerless. Where was their spiritual strength? After all they were Jesus's disciples.

Jesus told them, *"Oh faithless and perverse generation how long shall I be with you?"*

Afterward Jesus himself cast out the devil, and the child was cured. The disciples came to Jesus, and they asked him why they were unable to cast the demonic spirit out.

Jesus responded, "Because of your unbelief." The NIV uses these words, "Because you have so little faith." You should know my brothers and

[11] Charles Haddon Spurgeon

sisters that it is not enough to say that you believe in God. Just as it's not enough to just "show up" to church on Sundays. You must have a faith in God that you live out daily. For we walk by faith and not by sight. We must not be satisfied with where we are today spiritually. Our faith must grow stronger.

Scripture tells us that faith comes by hearing and hearing by the Word of God. Are we hearing God's Word? Are the scriptures becoming alive in our lives?

We cannot have a powerful Word if we are not men and women of faith. And we cannot be men and women of faith if we don't have God's words abiding in our hearts. That's why Bible class and Sunday school are essential in a Christian's growth. Do you see the connection? If you are a person of faith, then you should know that faith has the ability to bring about change.

Years ago when I was new to the ministry, I would go to the hospital to visit someone with a sense of hesitation and uncertainty. I wasn't quite sure what God would do. I didn't understand the power that God gives to those who serve him.

However, now when I go to the hospital, I'm not going wondering if God can heal. But rather, "Is it God's will that he uses me to heal?" God can do all things!

The disciples needed faith if they were to be like Christ. The disciples needed unwavering and courageous faith if they were going to have a powerful word.

After Jesus healed the man who was possessed with the devil, the people were amazed. They were in awe, impressed, and overwhelmed. They talked amongst themselves and said, "What a word is this!" It was with authority and power that Jesus commanded the unclean spirits, and they came out.

My brothers and sisters, we need to have spiritual power in days like these. We need to have a powerful word. Not so that people can lift us up and praise us, but we need to have a powerful word in order to bring someone to Christ.

We need to have a powerful word so we can convince the person that is going down the wrong road and doing the wrong things that Jesus still loves them and can help them turn their life around.

We need to have a powerful word to convince our brothers and sisters and our mothers and fathers that they should give their life to Christ. We need to have a powerful word that we can use to tell the devil when he's attacking us, "In the mighty name of Jesus, get behind me."

We need a powerful word when our loved ones get sick, we can call on the Lord, and he will raise them up. We need to have a powerful word so we can tell the world that Jesus is the way, the truth, and the life. We need to have a powerful word so we can tell the story that Jesus came into this world. We need to tell somebody that it was amazing grace that saved us.

Sermon 3: The Reality of the Fig Tree, "Fig Tree Faith" (Matthew 21:18–22)

Jesus our Christ and Lord was both human and divine at the same time. He possessed all of the qualities of the Father, and he was fully human. We know that Jesus was God when John the beloved disciple says, "In the beginning was the Word and the Word was with God and the word was God." Jesus was the Word of God.

Also Mathew tells us in Matthew 1:23, "Behold, the virgin shall conceive and bear a son, and they shall call his name Immanuel" (which means "God with us").

And Paul the apostle says in Colossians 1:15–16, "He is the image of the invisible God, the firstborn of all creation. For by him all things were created, in heaven and on earth, visible and invisible, whether thrones or dominions or rulers or authorities—all things were created through him and for him."

Jesus was God, but he was also human. He was a man who walked the face of this earth. Because he was human, he had five senses. He could see, smell, touch, taste, and hear.

Jesus became a man. John says in John 1:14, "And the Word was made flesh, and dwelt among us, (and we beheld his glory, the glory as of the only begotten of the Father,) full of grace and truth." Jesus was human. He got thirsty. In John 4, Jesus told the Samaritan woman to draw him some water. Also while on the cross, Jesus said, "I thirst."

Jesus shed tears and cried. At the grave site of his good friend, Lazarus, scripture says that Jesus wept. Jesus had to rest and sleep. Matthew 8:24 states, "And behold, there arose a great storm on the sea, so that the boat was being swamped by the waves; but he was asleep" (John 19:28).

We also learn in this text that Jesus was hungry. The Word says, "Now in the morning as he returned into the city, he hungered." He physically desired to have food. And this makes me think about what our Savior said in Matthew 5:6, "Blessed are they which do hunger and thirst after righteousness: for they shall be filled."

My brothers and sisters, we must have a spiritual hunger. We should have a hunger and thirst to please God. We must have a desire to walk after God's righteousness.

We're living in a generation where some Christians are trying to do just the minimum to get by. They have lost their zeal in serving the Lord. Worship and fellowship are not important to them.

When I worked for the government, there was a time when I had to supervise several new employees. We were working on a special statewide project, and I could tell the staff that really wanted to do their job from those who just wanted to do enough to get by. Some of them did not want to follow instructions on how to do their job. Others took the initiative to learn as much as they could so they could do their best.

Don't let Satan take your joy of worship away. Keep a spirit of hungering and thirsting after righteousness. The Lord says you shall be filled. Jesus was indeed physically hungry, and he was with his disciples during his last week of his earthly ministry. It was on a Monday, the day after Palm Sunday, that Jesus and his disciples were walking toward Jerusalem. The text says, "He saw a fig tree in the way. He came to it and found nothing thereon, but leaves only, and said unto it, 'Let no fruit grow on thee henceforward forever'. And presently the fig tree withered away."

As we read this verse in Matthew 21, we must also read what Mark 11 says. Similarly Mark tells us that Jesus saw a fig tree with only leaves on it. There were no figs on it. We learn from Mark's account that it wasn't the time of season to have figs on the tree.

Then Jesus curses the fig tree. Both accounts say that he cursed the fig tree. We learn from Matthew, "The fig tree withered at once." Mark tells us it was the next day that the disciples noticed that the fig tree had withered away. It is possible that some of the disciples noticed the tree withered away immediately and others the next day.

Listen to Jesus's powerful words. "'May no fruit ever come from you again!' And the fig tree withered at once" (Matthew 21:19). Some scholars tell us that cursing the fig tree was a symbolic act of God's rejection of unbelieving Israel. The Jews had no good fruit in their lives. They were spiritually barren. Yet no matter what the symbolic reason, the reality was that the fig tree became dry and wasted away as a direct result of the power of Jesus's words.

Jesus's words commanded authority. God's Word has authority. Isaiah the prophet says it like this, "So shall my word be that goes out from my mouth; it shall not return to me empty, but it shall accomplish that which I purpose, and shall succeed in the thing for which I sent it" (Isaiah 55:11).

In addition, Matthew 17:18–20 states,

> And Jesus rebuked the demon, and it came out of him, and the boy was healed instantly. Then the disciples came to Jesus privately and said, "Why could we not cast it out?" He said to them, "Because of your little faith. For truly, I say to you, if you have faith like a grain of mustard seed, you will say to this mountain, 'Move from here to there,' and it will move, and nothing will be impossible for you."

Jesus cursed a real fig tree. The fig tree was real, just like the Red Sea in Moses' day. The fig tree was real, just like the two fish and five loads. The fig tree was a real, just like the rock that Moses spoke to and water came out of it. The fig tree was real, just like the donkey who spoke to the false prophet and saved his life in Numbers 22. The reality of the fig tree means that it was something tangible, physical, and of real substance.

Notice that the disciples marveled at what they saw. The text says, "And when the disciples saw it, they marveled, saying, How soon is the fig tree withered away!"

It's amazing to me that the disciples were surprised or stunned at what they saw. They had been eyewitnesses to Jesus's other mighty miracles. Some of us today don't believe that God can still do great things.

Jesus' words still command power in the twenty-first century. Jesus still has all authority. Jesus states in Matthew 24:35, "Heaven and earth shall pass away, but my words shall not pass away." If the Lord has told you something, you must hold on to it.

How many of you believe God can do all things? God can do all things. God can do the impossible! He can give you a better job. He can take your little money and bless you with a better house or apartment. He can take your broken relationship and reconcile you back to your brother or sister. The reality of Jesus's words is that whatever he says will come to pass.

Jesus further states in the text, "Truly, I say to you, if you have faith and do not doubt, you will not only do what has been done to the fig tree, but even if you say to this mountain, 'Be taken up and thrown into the sea,' it will happen" (Matthew 21:21).

We must learn how to grow in our faith. We must learn how to operate our lives by faith.

Jesus told his disciples that if they have faith, they too could do the same thing to the fig tree. I believe Jesus was referring to a real fig tree. They could have fig tree faith.

If you don't believe you can curse a real fig tree at the command of your words and it will dry up, it won't happen. If you doubt your ability to do it, it will not occur.

Doubt is an enemy of faith. Doubt is a killer of faith. Doubt will stop your blessings from coming. Doubt will stop you from having fig tree faith. You must have power in your words.

James 1:6 says, "But let him ask in faith, with no doubting, for the one who doubts is like a wave of the sea that is driven and tossed by the wind." Likewise, Paul states, "I can do all things through him who strengthens me" (Philippians 4:13). John further states, "For he who is in you is greater than he who is in the world" (1 John 4:4).

Because of faith, we have power to curse the fig tree and also move mountains. Therefore, we must use our operational faith every day.

Utilizing operational faith is connected to the Word of God. Operational faith commands power that commands change. Operational faith gets its power from God's Word.

The apostle John records Jesus's words, "If you ask me anything in my name, I will do it" (John 14:14). 1 John 5:14–15 says, "And this is the confidence that we have toward him, that if we ask anything according to his will he hears us. And if we know that he hears us in whatever we ask, we know that we have the requests that we have asked of him."

Can you hear Jesus say to his disciples, "And whatever you ask in prayer, you will receive, if you have faith" (Matthew 21:22)? I'm so glad that Jesus will hear our prayer today.

Do you believe that Jesus can do all things?

Printed in the United States
By Bookmasters